Kyoto Machiya
Restaurant Guide

Kyoto Machiya Restaurant Guide

AFFORDABLE DINING
IN TRADITIONAL
TOWNHOUSE SPACES

Judith Clancy
Photographs by Ben Simmons

Stone Bridge Press • *Berkeley, California*

Published by
Stone Bridge Press
P.O. Box 8208, Berkeley, CA 94707
510-524-8732 • sbp@stonebridge.com • www.stonebridge.com

This book is dedicated to Jeanne Platt, a hardworking editor and our beloved colleague.

Text ©2012 Judith Clancy.

Cover illustration by Clifton Karhu.

Maps by Sumiya Toshio.

Photographs pp. 39–80 ©2012 Ben Simmons, www.bensimmonsphoto.com.

Restaurant entrance photographs pp. 3–38 (filtered) and pp. 82–248 by John Goodman and Allan Mandell.

Book design and layout by Linda Ronan.

Printed in the United States of America.

10 9 8 7 6 5 4 3 2 1   2016 2015 2014 2013 2012

This publication is also available as an e-book: ISBN 978-1-61172-549-0.

LIBRARY OF CONGRESS CATALOGING-IN-PUBLICATION DATA
Clancy, Judith.
    Kyoto machiya restaurant guide : affordable dining in traditional townhouse spaces / Judith Clancy ; photographs by Ben Simmons.
        p. cm.
    ISBN 978-1-61172-001-3 (pbk); ISBN 978-1-61172-549-0 (ebk).
1. Restaurants—Japan—Kyoto—Guidebooks. 2. Row houses—Japan—Kyoto—Guidebooks. 3. Kyoto (Japan)—Guidebooks. 4. Row houses—Japan—Kyoto—Pictorial works. 5. Wooden-frame buildings—Japan—Kyoto—Pictorial works. 6. Historic buildings—Japan—Kyoto—Pictorial works. 7. Architecture, Domestic—Japan—Kyoto—Pictorial works. 8. Kyoto (Japan)—Pictorial works. I. Simmons, Ben. II. Title.
    TX910.J3C55 2011
    647.9552'1864—dc23
                        2011029748

Contents

Introduction

For centuries, the beauty and humanity sustained within Kyoto's *machiya* (townhouses) have nurtured many a citizen, artist, craftsman, and entrepreneur. The measured space of these iconic wooden buildings—with their geometrical lattice designs, soft natural light, and corresponding shadows—is now part of the Japanese psyche. When visitors step inside, they will see a unique style of architecture, and they can look into the soul of Japanese society.

Through the first half of the 20th century, dozens of these buildings sat along narrow city streets, some as row houses and others with barely 10 cm (5″) between them.

Japan's desire to show the world and itself as a "modern" postwar society meant destroying this gracious, traditional architecture and replacing it with unsightly boxy concrete buildings. Yet by the end of the century, a little more than a decade ago, people began to reject the simply new and to cherish instead the disappearing roof lines, the intimacy of neighborhoods, and the intricate interplay of material and motif. The machiya, so much identified with the charming face of Kyoto, began garnering some of the respect they deserve.

Of course, technology has helped save these old buildings and foster some of the traditional lifestyle they nurture. Improved plumbing, heated flooring, and well-lit modern kitchens blend the grace of the old with the convenience and comfort of the new. Although flammable, these post-and-beam structures are resilient: Their ability to endure for centuries and withstand earthquakes has drawn modern builders to study old construction techniques and incorporate the best features into new homes.

Businesses also have recognized the benefits of renovating townhouses. Some are drawn by the financial benefits, others by the potential charms of the interiors. The buildings' settled and handsome façades add panache to merchandise displayed at street-level entrances, enticing passersby into an interior where the pleasure of lingering, eating—and shopping—is no less apparent for being subtle. More than two hundred newly established small restaurants and cafés, as well as shops specializing in traditional crafts, have joined the trend and taken over and repurposed old midtown homes.

Food, always a passion in Japan, has become a pop culture phenomenon. Japanese devotedly watch their TV food programs and hold their chefs in high esteem. Opening a restaurant has a glamorous appeal, and young entrepreneurs are making their mark. Japanese will mostly favor the taste of their latest food find over the atmosphere where it is served, but that is changing.

In the softly lit traditional settings of machiya, conviviality is assured—but not without a few changes to suit the changing times. The traditional tatami mat floor on which people sit cross-legged (men) or kneel (women) is often removed, since most Japanese now prefer to dine sitting on chairs. Some of the very exclusive, traditional restaurants that still retain tatami floors have installed a sunken area below the table that lets customers sit on the tatami while their feet rest on flooring below, encouraging them to linger longer and more comfortably over their repast. Sitting at floor level allows customers to enjoy the beauty of the inner gardens, which were built to be appreciated from that lower perspective. Many features are sacrificed to accommodate modern building regulations and spatial needs, but all the places that claim to be old townhouses have at least retained the traditional floor plan and an inner garden.

Modern renovation has gone a long way toward banishing the machiya's traditional image as a dark space made dank by an interior pump or well, musty tatami mats, and uninvited small creatures. The machiya's new image, portrayed in glossy magazines, is rich in shades of light and shadow and conveys a warm intimacy. Beautifully hewn beams and alcoves glow with indirect lighting splayed across displayed treasures, and, of course, satisfied customers are pictured dining, chopsticks or fork held delicately above artfully arrayed food.

ABOUT THE RESTAURANTS IN THIS BOOK

The restaurants and cafés listed in this book give readers a carefully selected portion of Kyoto's machiya. They have been chosen because they exhibit characteristics typical of the old townhouses and because their atmosphere is genuinely inviting. Even though their setting is quintessentially Japanese, a surprising number of restaurants offer very popular Italian or French cuisine, as well as Thai, Korean, or Chinese food. Café food ranges from a simple sandwich to fish and meat dishes, often with a well-stocked selection of cakes, as well as usually excellent coffee, espresso, or cappuccino.

I have mostly listed lunch menus that feature reasonably priced meals in a rich setting. Because night prices in the finer restaurants are rather expensive, I have omitted the many establishments that only open after 5:00 pm. You should not hesitate to try them, but the bill may be a bit of a surprise, especially if the meal is accompanied by alcohol. Since restaurants change management and options, it's a good idea—and perfectly acceptable—to call ahead and check on the price for the "lunch course."

You can order à la carte, but most restaurants and cafés offer *higawari*—a daily special, usually an appetizer or soup, a choice of main dish, and coffee or tea. The daily menus are always changing, and most Japanese rely on the chef to offer what is seasonal and on hand. It is not customary to ask for substitutions. If you have a serious allergy, just say so, and it will be removed from your serving.

Although some places have English menus, don't be deterred from going to those that don't. Prices are reasonable enough, and some of the staff may be able to explain the menu. The adventuresome and even not-so-adventuresome eater will be pleased with the food and the congenial atmosphere.

The restaurants in this guidebook specify the type of cuisine available, but even so, diners' expectations will differ—hopefully with pleasant results. Japanese chefs are ingenious and skillful, and their unique combination of ingredients and artful presentation will satisfy and delight many a gourmet.

TYPES OF JAPANESE RESTAURANTS

Japanese cuisine is remarkably diverse and just as remarkably unknown to many non-Japanese. Diners should expect specialization: no fish dishes at a noodle shop, no fried noodles at a sushi restaurant. The equipment, knives, utensils, dishes, and serving ware all have specific functions related to specific foods. If you want steak and your dining companion wants fish, only a family restaurant will satisfy both of you. These restaurants are proliferating and are particularly popular with families with young children.

For example, noodle dishes are served in *menrui,* noodle eateries, and even among noodle dishes, *soba* restaurants often feature just buckwheat noodles, and nothing else—not even wheat flour *udon* noodles. Ramen, a curly wheat-based noodle, is the preserve of inexpensive Chinese-style noodle shops; often open late at night, these eateries snare hungry and tipsy office workers on their way home.

Another nighttime-only restaurant is the *izakaya*, a Japanese pub where drinks accompany food, often *ippin-ryori* (one item per dish): a single plate of grilled mushrooms, *miso*-paste-topped tofu, or a filet of fish. The seasonal items are written on a blackboard or on strips of paper hanging on the wall. All the listed items are so familiar to Japanese throughout the country that no explanation is necessary, and the more popular dishes are often served with little regional variety.

Teppan-yaki means "iron-plate cooking" and refers to restaurants that serve a large variety of grilled foods, the most famous of which is *yakisoba* (fried noodles), closely followed in popularity by *okonomiyaki,* vegetable- and meat-filled pancakes you cook yourself at small restaurants with grills built into their tables.

Eateries serving *donburi* (literally, "big china bowl"), feature rice dishes topped with various ingredients.

Sushi restaurants only cater to that cuisine and never serve noodles.

Tofu (soy bean curd) restaurants, often located near temples, mostly feature a tofu-based vegetarian cuisine known as *shojin-ryori*.

Oden is a winter specialty comprising a large variety of seasonal vegetables, pork-stuffed buns, and eggs boiling away in a steaming and fragrant broth. The diner selects a few items, dabs on a bit of spicy mustard, and savors the warmth and camaraderie of the usually tiny eateries where *oden* is served.

Nabe-ryori (hot-pot cooking) serves up a variety of vegetables and meat, fish, or chicken in thick, shallow clay pots.

Sukiyaki and *shabu-shabu* (an onomatopoetic rendering of the sound of a slice of meat swished through boiling broth) restaurants serve beef, usually of high quality.

Kaiseki, the most refined and traditional of Japanese cuisine, is an array of set courses, all seasonally based and leisurely presented in a time-honored fashion. Originally, *kaiseki* referred to a warmed stone that monks placed in their *obi* (sashes) to suppress hunger pangs. Later it developed into a simple meal served with powdered green tea in a *chaji*, a ceremony lasting four hours. Today, *kaiseki* may be the most elaborate and expensive meal in town.

DINING ETIQUETTE

Here are some etiquette suggestions for dealing with some of the aspects that may be a bit unfamiliar to you in a Japanese restaurant. The best advice is to look around you and watch how other Japanese diners behave.

Much dining etiquette revolves around the use of chopsticks (*ohashi*; "honorable chopsticks," to be exact). These wooden utensils are often enclosed in a paper cover. After removing the cover, pull them apart if attached and rest them on the paper cover or the serving tray or dish.

When their food is served, Japanese will fold their hands in prayer, chopsticks resting in their thumbs, and say, *Itadakimasu* ("I humbly receive this"), an expression of thanks to all those involved in producing the meal, from the farmer who planted the seed and harvested the crop to the chef who prepared the finished product.

Use your chopsticks to stir the *miso* soup. Picking up your soup bowl and sipping from it is perfectly acceptable. You can also lift your rice bowl so that you are almost shoveling rice into your mouth. As there are no napkins in most restaurants, lifting the bowl to your mouth helps you avoid spills that would stain your clothing. While pausing between bites, rest your chopsticks on the edge of a dish or on the tray, but never leave them sticking directly into a bowl of rice (this is only done at the funeral repast, where the placesetting for the recently departed has the chopsticks set upright in the rice, making it easier for the dead spirit to partake).

Never pass food from chopstick to chopstick or use your chopsticks to transfer food directly from a "family style" serving dish to your mouth. To transfer food from a common dish to your plate, use the pair of chopsticks that should be resting on the common dish. If there are no extra chopsticks available, use the reverse end of your chopsticks. Never use the end that you have put in your mouth or attempt to lick the tips of your chopsticks clean.

If you drop any eating utensil, signal the waiter by saying *Sumimasen* ("Excuse me") and hold up the dropped item. It will be quickly replaced. Do not wipe it off with the wet towel provided for washing your hands.

Raw fish is one of the first dishes served at a meal of traditional Japanese cuisine (*kaiseki*). Put a bit of horseradish (*wasabi*) in the tiny dish containing soy sauce (*shoyu*), lightly dip the piece of raw fish into the mixture (do not bathe it in sauce), and savor. Grated radish is often served with tempura; put the radish into the broth and dip the tempura into it.

In traditional meals, rice is served last with pickles, after which, a slice of fruit might be served (nowadays some *kaiseki* restaurants even serve pudding or green tea ice cream).

When food is served on a tray and you wish to indicate that you are finished eating, lay your chopsticks directly on the tray or return them halfway into their paper cover and fold over the end of the cover to show they have been used and can be discarded.

When leaving the table, if you are seated on the floor, do not step on or over the seat cushions; step around them as well as other diners' extended legs or belongings that are in your way.

When you want to use the restroom, if you are not sure whether it is occupied, knock. If you are answered with a knock, stand and wait, or return to your seat until you see that the facility is empty.

Lastly, do not be embarrassed to ask which sauce goes with which dish, or when a hot-pot dish is ready after the flame under it has been lit, or for an extra bowl of rice. The staff will be glad to explain eating procedures and help you with any difficulties.

You may also notice the same assistance being given to the Japanese customers.

HOW TO USE THIS BOOK

Visitors to Kyoto, most of them armed with maps and on their way to some of the city's renowned temples and shrines, pass by fine examples of indigenous architecture not shown on any guidebook map. Until the end of the last century, these machiya were private residences, but as the population has aged and property has changed hands, many of these structures have been converted into beautiful restaurants, cafés, and shops. This book was written for those who wish to have a fulfilling meal in these interesting, traditional settings.

Following an introduction to machiya culture is a photo essay by accomplished photographer Ben Simmons to attune the eye to the subtle beauty of these structures. These sections will enhance your dining experience and give you information about the unique characteristics of Japanese residences.

The guidebook section introduces you to over 140 restaurants within converted machiya and historic buildings. These are grouped within chapters organized by district and listed alphabetically. To find what district of Kyoto you are in and its corresponding restaurant, use the Map and District Locator map on pages 82–83. Then use the appropriate map on the indicated page. On maps C, D, and F are approximately 80 restaurants within a 5-to-20-minute walk apart. Other areas of Kyoto are introduced as well, so you can enjoy a meal without returning to the main streets of the city. (Map H actually covers three separate outlying districts of Kyoto, grouped together for convenience.)

Restaurants are also listed by name and by cuisine in the indexes in the back of the book. (Much of the cuisine is a fusion of culture and local ingredients, so the listings should be used as an indicator of a type of cuisine rather than a definitive description. Most all of the chefs are Japanese.)

You can also just open the book and find a restaurant that interests you by reading the brief description of its architecture, history, and food. The highlights and distinguishing characteristics of each restaurant are described in order to enhance your dining experience. There is always a lot to notice, from furnishings to architectural elements, including window types, floors, stairwells, and the treatment of overhead beams, posts, and transoms. Names of Japanese people are given in Japanese order, that is, family name first.

The machiya restaurants within the guide are all inexpensive to moderately priced, so there is no price-ranking scheme. In general, if you want to sample the food and save money, avoid dinner hours. Food in these restaurants is prepared to order using fresh ingredients, served on varied dinnerware, so it may be more expensive than in restaurant chains, but tipping is not necessary and most machiya restaurants do not include a service charge. However, many of the small places accept only cash.

Each restaurant is identified by its name in Roman letters (mostly using the restaurant's preferred spelling), followed by its name in Japanese. A letter-numeral combination tells you its location on the map. Thus, B3 indicates restaurant #3 on Map B (generally, the numbers on each map move from north to south and east to west, so close numbers usually indicate geographical proximity). At the end of each restaurant entry are hours, location, and other details, all indicated by the following icons:

➡️ Walking directions or street location. Use these with the photographs of the restaurant entrances to help in street-level identification.

🕐 Hours of operation. Some restaurants close after lunch and open again for dinner. "LO" = "last order"; the restaurant usually stays open a little later than that to allow diners to finish. Day closures and holiday hours are noted here. Be aware that hours and closure days can change at any time. Unlike established chain restaurants, most of these machiya restaurants are small and often owned by the people serving you (which is part of their charm).

📞 Phone number. If you are calling from a cell phone, include the Kyoto area code 075; otherwise just use the 7-digit number. Few staff will be able to conduct an extended conversation in English. If you are worried, ask your hotel concierge or a friend to call and inquire about hours, prices, or reservations, but just dropping in is perfectly fine.

rsvp Reservations, when recommended.

@ Website, if there is one. Most machiya websites are in Japanese, although some provide an English-language section. Online you can usually find a map and color photographs of the food and interior. Some online English-language travel guides include these same restaurants with up-to-date hours, maps, and transportation notes.

🚗 Address in Japanese. Just show this to your taxi

driver and he will be able to find the restaurant. (Sometimes the text here shows an actual area address, and other times it is directional, since many Kyoto streets are unnamed. The locals understand this so you needn't worry. The suffix -*dori* means "street" and is often dropped.)

Machiya establishments represent a commitment by their owners to preserve an important architectural legacy. Some restaurants may go out of business or change hands (and cuisines) after this book has been published. There are pages at the end of the book for you to note any new finds and add your personal remarks. The publisher welcomes your comments and updates to include them in the next print edition and in the more easily revised e-book editions.

WHERE DO I START? A LIST OF PERSONAL FAVORITES

I asked my dining companions for their top 10 favorite restaurants and cafés, places that have an interesting menu, a congenial atmosphere, a reasonable price, and good service. There was so much variation in their choices, that the list grew to 20. Here, in alphabetical order, are their picks. Start with any of these, all listed in this guide, and you simply can't go wrong:

Amore, Ao, Café Chocolat, Casa Bianca, Gogyo, Juga, Kushikura, Mametora, Meirin, Misato, O-mo-ya Higashinotoin, Pasta Collection House Dogetsu, Robinson, Sagano-yu, Sarasa Nishijin, Sobadokoro Sasaya, Sumire, Ristorante t.v.b, Takara, Zezekan Pocchiri

Acknowledgments

Food preferences vary, so I have asked some friends to accompany me on my gastronomical forays. Their opinions helped evaluate many of the factors that went into making a selection. For this I wish to thank Akai Naomi, Egawa Hiroko, Fujimoto Harumi, Fujiso Nobuko, Hayashi Hiroko, Konno Kazuyo, Dr. Okada Tatehiko, Ofune Akiko, and Yamaoka Hitoshi. Hayashi Hiroko completed the onerous task of checking addresses and names and did so with her usual graceful capability.

Kotani Sadako and Oki Michi helped confirm information I had gathered or had learned from hearsay. Ashida Tomohide and Ayumi Ikushima introduced me to several places and their staff. Dr. Tomoyoshi Eiko helped confirm facts and gave her valuable opinion about Japanese culture. Kinoshita Ryoichi advised me concerning structural differences between townhouses in cities other than Kyoto.

I am very indebted to long-time Kyoto resident John E. Goodman, who photographed the entrances (unless otherwise credited, he took most of the façade photos). Allan Mandell, artist and garden photographer, helped take last-minute photos of restaurants that had changed their names or façades.

Ben Simmons's artistic eye captured the subtle allure of Kyoto's beautiful machiya, helping to visually distill the essence of the city's architecture.

The manuscript needed reading, which Terry Allen, a former resident of Japan, kindly agreed to do, and it is through her skill and good humor that the task was completed.

Marc Keane, author of *Japanese Garden Design* and many other books on Japanese gardens, was extremely generous with his time and knowledge of Japanese architecture and gardens to graciously read, edit, and make invaluable suggestions. Riyo Tsujino, a forest ecologist at the Research Institute for Humanity and Nature in Kyoto, gave me advice about the section on wood, as did Mechtild Mertz, an associate researcher at the East Asia Civilisations Research Centre, Paris. Sumiya Toshio had the unenviable job of turning my scribble into maps; to complete the guide, he added alleyways that exist on few city maps.

A very special thanks to a long-time friend, Lois Karhu, who suggested that I use one of Clif Karhu's prints for the cover. The legacy of Clif's love of Kyoto continues to impress me.

The hardworking and under-appreciated staff at the Kyoto Center of Community Collaboration gave me their cooperation whenever I needed it.

To Peter Goodman, the publisher, and his very patient and persevering staff, many thanks for helping this project reach the readers' hands and offering readers the opportunity to learn a little about this venerable architectural heritage.

I wish to dedicate this book to Jeanne Platt, and the special joy she brought to this project through her enthusiastic and capable editing.

Kyoto
Machiya
Restaurant
Guide

Machiya Culture

THE DEVELOPMENT OF THE CITY

The tale of any city is distilled through its architecture. Many fine examples of traditional structures that bespeak Kyoto's long and rich history are still located on the streets of this old capital.

In the Heian period (794–1185), the layout of the city's boulevards and sectioned neighborhood blocks, or *cho*, made Kyoto one of the grandest city-planning ventures of its time. It became the city of the imperial court: home to emperors and aristocrats, and later to warlords, artisans, craftsmen, and commoners, whose needs impressed themselves upon the city design.

Geomancers were called upon to pronounce their interpretation of yin and yang (*inyo gogyo*), after which streets were set in perfectly straight lines within a grid on a north-south axis with a south-facing palace. These ancient streets still exist, narrowed in some cases, merged with others, but many with the original names that became monikers of ancient families, such as Karasuma, Nijo, or Konoe, or that named the different trades being practiced, such as Ayakoji (Twill Street) for its fine fabric weave and Kiyamachi (Wood Shop Street) for its business of selling and transporting lumber and charcoal.

Within this grid, property was divided into large blocks, modeled on the ancient Chinese city of Chang'an (modern X'ian). Courtiers were allotted property according to their rank. Their compounds were enclosed by high earthen walls. Within were extensive one-storied buildings set on low pillars connected by passageways interwoven with streams, ponds, and greenery. The nobility loved their gardens. Visual access to them year round was an important part of their aesthetic sensitivity and became an enduring cultural value in Japan. Building materials were wood, earth, and paper. (Stone construction was not common until castles were built in the middle ages, and even then, stonework was confined to the foundation's retaining walls—the outer walls of a castle were thick clay.) Tile roofs were limited to temples; other dwellings were covered by bark, shingles, or boards. Little metal was used in basic construction but occasionally served as decorative detail on door pulls or nail covers.

Wells supplied most of the water. A system of gutters channeled water from the Otowa, Takano, Kamo, Katsura, and Shirakawa rivers through the city, carrying away discarded laundry water. Toilets were placed over huge clay pots, whose contents were sold to farmers for fertilizer.

This was Kyoto in its early years. Various accounts estimate the population expanded from 80,000 when it was founded in 874 to about 130,000 in the 10th century.

Commoners had their very modest abodes in and around the grand estates, and fields and vegetable patches were located around the periphery. Even today, neat vegetable patches can be found near Kamigamo Shrine in the northern part of the city where farmers pickle their produce in wooden containers weighted closed with suspended stones and in the southwest where vegetable stands dot the roadsides with only a little box for the buyer to leave payment.

Detail from the exterior of the restaurant Omuraya.

From the 11th to 14th centuries, wars, natural disasters, and the rise of militant groups fighting for territory destroyed great swaths of the city. The capital was moved to Kamakura, several hundred miles to the northeast (south of what is now Yokohama) by the shogun Minamoto no Yoritomo, and during this Kamakura period (1185–1333) parts of Kyoto succumbed to neglect and became desolate.

The emperor at that time, Go Daigo, returned to Kyoto but again fled the city when his military advisor, Ashikaga Takauji, came into power. During the Muromachi period (1336–1573), the capital revived, allowing a great number of tradesmen and artisans to flourish (or, depending on how one views history, the city revived because the tradesmen flourished). The Ashikaga family supported the arts, and the city slowly began to overcome decades of neglect and poverty.

Eleven years of fighting during the Onin War (1467–77) again reduced many buildings to rubble, and citizens gravitated to two fortifications: the Upper fort known as Kamigyo no Kamae and the Lower, Shimogyo no Kamae. The housing within these two districts was grouped around the large estates belonging to the military or aristocrats. Only one street connected them: Muromachi-dori. Kyoto's face had greatly changed.

With the need to insure the growth of the capital, former restrictions on land use lessened. Homes of commoners and merchants were allowed to sit next to or very near those of high-ranking military officers and nobility. The original grand *cho* were gradually broken into smaller estates, or, in the case of areas occupied by commoners, side streets and alleys appeared. The definition of a *cho* shifted from a block bordered by four streets to a set of houses that faced each other across a street; sometimes these streets and alleys remained unnamed (this is true even today). Shops crowded both sides of the roads to meet the growing demand for goods, allowing the merchant class to expand. By the 16th century, prototypes of today's townhouses started to be constructed as merchants grew wealthy. Temples were rebuilt and repaired, shrines were erected, and businesses had to tend not only to the needs of Kyoto's citizens but also to the many pilgrims swarming in to visit its temples. Entertainment districts developed, and festivals became a popular event for neighborhood associations, a chance to carouse and honor the gods at the same time.

In 1568, the warlord Oda Nobunaga (1534–84) entered Kyoto and began to govern. His untimely assassination brought into power another warlord, Toyotomo Hideyoshi (1535–98), whose rule brought great changes to the city's physical layout. Hideyoshi undertook the immense project of enclosing the city with a large earthen embankment (*odoi*) that was completed in 1590. Entry points to the city were called *kuchi* or "mouths." Temples were built along the eastern perimeter as part of the defense (*teramachi*), streets were further realigned, temples destroyed during the fighting by Nobunaga were rebuilt, and bridges across the Kamo River were enlarged.

Hideyoshi eventually decided that this earthen wall did not insure a good enough defense of the city, so he built a castle in Momoyama on a rise in Fushimi to the south of the city center. Around the castle were the residences of his warriors (*buke-yashiki*) at the confluence of three rivers: the Uji, Kamo, and Katsura, well suited for trade with Osaka. Springs of clear delicious water, an essential ingredient of sake, were plentiful, and breweries flourished. Traders, boatsmen, sake makers, and entertainers joined the residing warriors to inhabit this river port. The turmoil of the preceding centuries was mostly over, and the city at this time assumed the shape it would maintain for several more centuries.

In the 17th century, an interesting architectural development emerged as a result of the association between the warlord Hideyoshi and Sen no Rikyu (1522–1647), son of a wealthy merchant from nearby Sakai City, who elevated the serving of green powdered tea into an art.

Green leaf tea had been imbibed as a medicinal stimulant from the 8th century; by the 13th century the leaves were being dried and ground into powder to produce *matcha* (green powdered tea). The act of drinking tea itself had become a ritual that favored special utensils and a rustic setting, a development from the days when the merchants of Sakai would gather after a refreshing bath to have a convivial bowl of tea in a country setting.

The decorative elements employed in the tea ritual ushered in the beginning of a distinctly Japanese aesthetic lexicon that is still very much in evidence today. The term *wabi* describes beauty of a simple rustic nature, a concept given form through the introduction of small intimate tearooms and tea houses with unobtrusive gardens, attractive thatched roofs, fine earthen and clay walls, wooden posts and beams of smoothed and polished wood, woven tatami mat flooring in rooms with paper-covered windows (*shoji*), and patterned-paper sliding doors (*fusuma*).

In itself, none of these elements was new, but their combination in the composition of a structure evoked the simple pleasures of an intimacy with nature: the scent of freshly scrubbed wood, the wind-in-the-pines whispering sound of water boiling in a good iron kettle, the deliberate scattering of cherry blossom petals or autumn leaves on a neatly swept pathway. The *tokonoma*, or alcove, is a recessed section of wall in which a scroll could be hung and flowers arranged to coordinate the seasonal theme as background to the tea ceremony.

So popular did the tea ceremony prove that the wealthier merchants and warrior classes often had a "rustic" thatched-roof tearoom or teahouse built on their property. The tea ceremony had become a main pastime of the upper classes, insuring its accompanying architectural heritage a permanent place in Japanese society.

In the Edo period (1615–1868), after the defeat of Hideyoshi's son, the Tokugawa shogunate controlled almost every aspect of daily life. Rigid social ranks were designated, and society was divided into four descending levels: warriors, farmers, artisans, and merchants. Housing was regulated according to one's rank, but the increasing wealth of the merchant class gave this lowest class the leeway to further refine and subtly elaborate traditional building styles.

The legacy of today's townhouses was thus seeded over the nearly three centuries of Tokugawa rule. During this time, Japan rebuffed all foreign trade and became isolated, cultivating an era of peace that allowed the merchant class to firmly establish itself. Rules were strictly enforced, and housing styles were codified as were those for clothing. Many of Kyoto's old structures date from this time, with newer ones copying their features.

The entrance to the restaurant Tsuki-tokage.

Townhouses lined the streets, the width of their frontage determining the amount of taxes assessed to their owners. Consequently, the houses tended to be long with narrow frontage. Since they were built so very close to one another, open space was left in the middle of the structure to install a garden that provided light and air to an otherwise dark interior. Inside, two distinctive sections took form: the front of the house with street access and its shop (*omoteya*), and the inner back rooms where the family lived (*omoya*).

A wooden lattice front allowed a bit of light to enter the shop and offered those within a limited view of passersby. Pedestrians could see into the front room but not into the interior of the shop.

Access was through a wooden door that customers or neighbors would slide open to vocally announce their presence (this is true even today; there are few doorbells). The entrance area consisted of dense packed dirt and later concrete or flat inlaid stones depending on the prosperity of the household.

Upon entering, customers would remove their shoes before stepping up to enter the raised, tatami-mat area. Business was conducted in this front area, whereas business of a personal nature or that with longstanding customers was done in an inner room affording more privacy.

The earthen floor formerly extended to the back of the house and its kitchen with its well or pump. The kitchen ceiling revealed the underside of the roof; a skylight was inserted to give this area a bit of light. The toilet and bath, where they existed, were next to the house, slightly apart from the structure proper.

Kimon, or unlucky directions, still play a part in the life of Kyoto inhabitants, so floor layout dictates that the northeast and southwest corners remain relatively free and open. Occasionally one sees cones of salt on the northeast corners of businesses, due to the belief that ill fortune comes from that direction, thus requiring the purifying qualities of salt.

These beliefs in unlucky directions still find a place in the architectural designs of new buildings, even more so in structures built up until a hundred years ago. Centuries of refinement, social restrictions, choice limitations of materials, the dictates of geomancy (fengshui), the great aesthetic appeal of the tea ceremony, and elements of the native faith of Shinto's respect for nature are all interwoven and today are embodied in Kyoto's architectural heritage.

THE EMERGENCE OF ARCHITECTURAL STYLES

Over the centuries, especially in its temples, Japan developed styles of architecture borrowed from China in the Tang dynasty (618–907). Through the exchange of official envoys to the continent from the mid-7th century, Japanese became aware of the grandeur of Chinese indigenous architecture. Chinese carpenters were sent for to oversee the construction of temples as Buddhism took root.

Chinese-style buildings of the time provided flexibility in earthquake-prone Japan: Their structural posts were set on foundation stones, and they had raised flooring. Beams met in elaborate joinery allowed tall structures such as pagodas to withstand the rippling and swaying ground. Later, with the development of iron foundries, nails and spikes were employed, but sparingly, hidden by attractive metal coverings. Low ornamental railings graced outer wooden verandas, rooms were divided by sliding paper doors (*fusuma*), and sloping tiled roofs extended overhanging eaves to deflect the heavy rains of June and July. All these features gradually became part of the developing native aesthetic.

Their flexibility allowed these wooden structures to expand in the humidity and shrink with age, insuring their survival. Only fire, war, and termites were their fatal enemies. The court noble Yoshida Kenko (128?-1359?) wrote that "homes should be built for summer. In the winter one can live anywhere, but dwellings unsuited to the hot months are unendurable." This of course mainly applies to the southern end of the Japanese archipelago. Curiously enough, many homes even in the northern districts seem to ignore the demands of a colder climate to a greater degree than those of neighboring countries—the warm *ondol* floors being a good example of how Koreans adapted to freezing weather. In areas far to the north of Kyoto, the desire to imitate buildings in the capital took precedence over comfort, and northern residents huddled around *irori* (open hearths) to keep warm when the snow piled up outside. (The city of Takayama in

Detail from the exterior of the restaurant Taotei.

Gifu Prefecture has many fine examples of huge homes whose main source of heat was a few lengths of charcoal and padded clothing.)

Shinto shrine construction eventually followed that of temples. Initially, the Shinto gods were worshipped in places of natural wonder: waterfalls, mountains, and groves of massive trees. Later, when it was deemed necessary to create a building to "house" the god, the main pillars were inserted directly into the earth. This practice, which required frequent replacement as the wood succumbed to rot, is still followed at the main Shinto shrine of Ise in Mie Prefecture and is one reason the shrine is rebuilt every 20 years.

Shinto shrines are distinguished by a simple open gate called a *torii*, often made of wood painted a vermilion color but occasionally of stone. The timber used for the shrine building is usually unvarnished and light colored. The shrine roof is shingled with cedar or cypress bark. The raised wooden structure has an inner altar containing a bronze mirror. Twisted straw ropes with strips of cut white paper are sometimes hung under the *torii* and denote the grounds as sacred, and sometimes a rock or a tree tied with a straw rope is given a place of honor within the precincts. More elaborate Shinto structures emerged in later centuries; the brightly colored 17th-century mausoleum of the Tokugawa shogun at Nikko (north of Tokyo) more resembles a Buddhist temple, reflecting the merging of innovative carpentry skills.

As aesthetics evolved, so did dwellings, reflecting people's expectations and their growing pocketbooks. The ideal house in Japan was one that incorporated the finishing touches introduced by the upper classes, and so, after 1,500 years, the Japanese love of highly refined simplicity continues to define their living quarters. Even a Western-style home or apartment building will contain one tatami room to accommodate overnight guests. It will have clay and plaster walls and glass windows with an inner paper window (*shoji*) and opaque, thicker paper sliding doors (*fusuma*).

Dwellings also reflected the type of city in which they were built: castle towns (*jokamachi*); those laid out around temples (*jinaicho*); and cities that thrived thanks to their granaries near waterways and ports (*minatomachi*). Kyoto with its castle, temples, shrines, old palaces, and homes of former courtiers contains a wealth of representative Japanese structures.

THE PRIMACY OF WOOD

The dense, shady forests of Japan's islands are a veritable wooded wonderland that supports a rich diversity of flora and fauna. Underbrush of ferns, bamboo grass, and *shaga* irises carpet the floor while birdsong sounds the high tones, the chatter of monkeys penetrate, and the retreating footsteps of serow and deer whisper their silent passage. Towering above this rich ecosystem are the massive treetops of beech, birch, black pine, camphor, cedar, cherry, chinkapin, cypress, elm, hackberry, hornbeam, horse chestnut, larch, magnolia, oak, paulownia, red pine, and zelkova, and thick groves of bamboo.

Over a millennium ago, the first inhabitants of this area

encountered colossal trees, some of which can still be seen in the girth of the pillars and beams of ancient Nara- and Heian-period temples. A seemingly endless supply of timber encouraged wood construction, and tools soon developed to allow the felling of even the largest of trees. As population expansion made more demands of the forests, mountains became denuded (*hageyama*), after which erosion caused much valuable topsoil to be lost and alluvial soil to flow into rivers, allowing the waters to rise and flood everything downstream. It became necessary to travel farther away to obtain the trees necessary to meet the demands of lumber for the new palaces, aristocratic residences, temples, and simple dwellings of the growing capital.

All parts of the tree were valued, and nothing was wasted, but the very nature of wood construction required frequent renewal from the damage caused by dampness or flame. Time and time again, the bark, twig, board, or thatched roofs were easily set aflame from cooking fires, destroying temple and grand villa alike as conflagrations swept through the city. With the advent of Buddhist temple construction in the 6th century, tile roofing was introduced. (Commoners did not have the means to tile their homes for over another thousand years.) Even though it took a lot of wood to fire the kilns, the durable clay roof tiles lasted longer, making the effort worth the expense—and eventually more affordable. However, even today, thatched roofed farmhouses can be seen in the countryside, evoking a sentimental response in Japanese who cherish their past. This aesthetic sentimentality is carried over into the tea ceremony; the thatched roof structures that exist in the city are mainly small teahouses.

The scarcity of lumber encouraged the construction of clay walls supported by a pliable grid framework of bamboo. Actually a grass, bamboo has remained a plentiful resource. A major change in dwelling interiors, fully manifest by the 17th century, was the use of a woven mat (tatami) made from rushes (*igusa*) to cover sections of the simple wooden plank floors of many homes.

By the 18th century, forest restoration was part of a government policy that allowed village woodcutters to replant and maintain designated mountainsides. Fast-growth trees, such as camphor, were used for carving rather than for house infrastructure, and zelkova became employed after the introduction of the ripsaw, which allowed the cutting of lengthwise planks. As the supply of large cypress trees became scarce, zelkova was increasingly used in the construction of large temples. Trees that grew straight, such as cypress and cedar, were preferred as a woodland "crop." The cedar could be harvested in 15 to 30 years, and the slower-growing cypress trees were left unfelled longer when very large logs were needed, sometimes up to 200 years. During this long growing period, the cypress forests had to be thinned again and again, and these smaller logs were used for various purposes, such as posts for roofs.

The faster-growing trees provided the woodsman's family with an income and ensured a stable supply of lumber, firewood, and leaf mulch. Three subgenera of oak (*kunugi, nara,* and *konara*) supplied charcoal production, another precious commodity, and a main source of cooking and heating fuel until the 20th century. In mountain areas not suitable for rice cultivation, or too far to practically transport timber, villages planted orchards of plum, apricot, peach, and, later, apple and fruit-bearing cherry trees. Land was carefully managed and maintained throughout the archipelago, so that today, the few stands of primordial forest that remain are in virtually inaccessible places.

Wooden pillar and gate at the entrance to The Oriental Garden.

As unfortunate as the disappearance of ancient forests was, Japan's forest management policy meant that mountains regained their woodland cover, making lumber available for homes and fuel obtainable for cooking. The younger trees harvested today exhibit a decline in girth, resulting in the smaller posts and beams seen in contemporary houses. Japan's love of wood is still great, but today's supplies come from new-growth forests or are imported, often from Southeast Asia but also from the northwest U.S. and Canada, and some even from Europe.

The reality of having a paucity of trees for building has honed the Japanese appreciation of wood to an inarguably high degree. The carpenter knows his market well, and trees are carefully selected to provide just the right quality: beautiful grain in floor planks at the entrance of a house or temple, an exotically angled main post in an alcove, the tactile feel of a sushi bar counter, or a decided fragrance for a bathtub or a lady's delicate hairpin.

When the carpenter visits a lumberyard, he casts a knowledgeable eye over the aged wood before him, assessing its durability, flexibility, and aesthetic value. Massive decades-old seasoned trees are handled with reverence and often earmarked to serve exclusively as replacements in temples and buildings designated as Important Cultural Properties. Respect for finely grained wood, and the beauty it offers, is a tacit component of Japanese culture.

Shinto shrines often have old-growth trees in their vicinity, encircled with a straw rope to signify their sacredness. Should any of these trees need to be felled, the work is done with due respect to the spirit of the tree; a small conical mound of salt is placed next to the stump, acknowledging the life taken, salt purifying the impurity of the death of a living organism.

To enter a traditional house is to be embraced by the love and dedication of the carpenter who labored there. Interior touches throughout emphasize the stunning beauty of unpainted wood skillfully buffed to a sheen. Complemented by fine earthen or plaster walls, the wooden beams and pillars picturesquely frame and nurture the aesthetic sensitivity of the craftsmen who produced the home and those who chose to live within it.

PRESERVING THE MACHIYA COMMUNITY

The word *machiya* literally means "townhouse," and in recent years it has come to signify an urban dwelling that evokes intimacy, warmth, soft natural light, and a sense of community. Constructed of wood, clay, and paper with space for an interior garden, the machiya dwelling embodies many of the aesthetic values inherent in Japanese culture. But this traditional structure is disappearing—a victim of age, building regulations, and benign neglect.

Scrolls depicting scenes from the late 12th century show the simple homes for laborers and the lower levels of society. These structures resemble row houses made with crudely cut planks of wood and simple wooden hanging windows that open out and are secured from above. The interior is tamped-down earth with a raised area for sleeping. The dwellings resemble a line of stalls, flimsy and easily replaceable. In contrast, the elaborate estates of the nobility as depicted in 17th-century scrolls are architectural works of art, aloof and elaborate, painted on a field of gold foil and pictured through parted clouds.

In the 6th century, building techniques and tools brought from China along with Buddhism introduced huge raised structures surrounded with corridors and handrails and rooms that opened onto landscaped grounds. The aristocracy then incorporated the spatial and structural aspects of temple design into their own dwellings. Sliding doors and standing screens that could be removed increased interior space. Pavilions and covered walkways were added as carpentry tools improved and tastes became more refined.

The estates of the aristocrats (their size depending on the rank of their owner) took up large lots within a *cho* (district), and smaller streets and alleys gradually intruded into them. Addresses in Kyoto are still defined by the *cho*, which represents more a demarcation than a street or house number; it is the bane of those seeking a particular house and a challenge to postal workers (thus giving a boost to modern electronic navigation systems!).

The rise of the merchant class in the 16th century necessitated larger shops and storehouses with street frontage to enable customer access. The family lived in the back of these long narrow dwellings—called an "eel's nest" (*unagi-no-nedoko*)—while the front rooms (*mise-no-ma*) were devoted to business. The homes engaged in business transactions (*shoka*) were larger than those of workers and remained in families for generations, even if it meant adopting a son-in-law to retain the name of the family and with it, its property. In July, many of these large dwellings open to visitors in the evenings preceding the Gion Festival, an event customarily supported by families in the textile business.

Detail from the exterior of the restaurant Kokoroya.

For centuries, until the beginning of the 19th century, simple wooden row houses (*minka*) were the abode of commoners. These buildings had a framework of wooden pillars and shared walls of clay or plaster, and, when affordable, tiles to replace plank-board roofs. The floors at the entrance and in the kitchen were packed earth, and there was a raised area with tatami mats over simple planked floors. The interior of the house was for sleeping and eating.

House owners tended to use local carpenters and gardeners to build and maintain their property, refining their façades and gradually bringing a uniformity to the alleys, streets, and interior gardens. This was especially true after sections of the city were destroyed by fire. Kyoto has a long history of destructive fires. The last massive one to sweep the city was in 1788, after which rapid reconstruction was essential. There was little time for innovative construction techniques, and the result was a uniformity in buildings that remained widespread until after WWII.

Centuries of refinement thus yielded the urban beauty of Kyoto streets up and into the 20th century. Homes of the working class maintained a tidy, simple charm with a communal pump or well for washing laundry. Public bathhouses allowed everyone to gather regularly to share news and watch their children grow, marry, and start families. A new baby was welcomed by all, and the needs of elders were a shared concern. Even today, those living in the old neighborhoods pay an annual fee to support their neighborhood associations (*chonaikai*), which pass along news via a clipboard of announcements of sporting and seasonal events, group walks and trips, health news, and shopping catalogs. In these close-knit neighborhoods, after the breakfast dishes are put away, housewives gather in the morning and in late afternoon for a chat, a bit of gossip, and sometimes to share the purchase of vegetables from farmers bringing their produce into the city from outlying areas.

Portable shrines are paraded through neighborhoods every spring and fall, stopping at designated houses to receive cash contributions and for the shrine bearers to receive refreshment. This neighborhood practice honors the gods and bestows another year of continued good health and prosperity on the participants while bonding the community.

The Jizo-bon Festival for children marks the end of summer

in late August. It is another gathering of neighbors, who clean the local image of Jizo (a Buddhist figure who protects children, pregnant women, and travelers). Neighbors welcome a Buddhist priest who prays before the statue, after which games and storytelling are organized for the children who live under that neighborhood shrine's guardianship. Newer

The courtyard at the entrance to the restaurant Ganko.

housing areas with young families continue the tradition by showing animated videos or organizing barbeques.

Yusuzumi is the word for sitting outside in the evening to cool oneself. Some old houses have fold-up benches attached to their front to serve that purpose. Elsewhere, people just bring out a chair to sit and enjoy a word with passersby, fanning themselves as evening descends with a welcome drop in temperature. These are some of the favorite images the old townhouse neighborhoods perpetuate and that are regularly featured on Japanese TV shows and in films.

Now these dwellings—with their great beam infrastructures, inner gardens, and raised flooring with tatami mats—are becoming scarcer, to the point of being considered somewhat exotic. "Newer is better" was the motto of postwar Japan when downtown wards were designated as commercial areas. Old buildings that needed renovating were replaced with concrete-box-type structures, and graceful roof lines disappeared along with their wooden façades and comely potted plants. The newer homes' private baths and washing machines lessened communal interaction. A way of life was disappearing, as was the craftsmanship needed to maintain it.

Kyotoites have now taken matters into their own hands and are trying as best they can to preserve their traditional residences. They often lose to inheritance tax obligations if the property is in a commercial zone, but otherwise they are doing an admirable job of preserving their architectural culture wherever they can. (Those inheriting property are often forced to sell it just to pay Japan's huge inheritance taxes. The building has little value; it is the land and its location that determine the price.)

In 1972, Kyoto adopted an ordinance to protect important landmarks and their vicinities: the weaving and dyeing district of Nishijin (south of Imadegawa-dori and west of Horikawa-dori), the area along the Kamo River, the foothills of Higashiyama, and the old castle site of Fushimi.

Several years later, four sections in popular tourist areas were designated Important Conservation Districts: Sannenzaka and Gion Shinbashi (1976), Saga Toriimoto (1979), and Kamigamo Shakemachi (1988).

In 1996, another ordinance introduced five categories for preservation:

- Aesthetic Zone (*bikan chiku*)
- Buildings and Townscape Adjustment Zone (*kenzobutsu shukei chiku*)
- Roadside Landscape Formations Zone (*endo keikan keisei chiku*)
- Historic Landscape Preservation Zone (*rekishiteki keikan hozen shukei chiku*)

- Historic Atmosphere Maintenance Zone (*kaiwai keikan seibi chiku*)

Much of the impetus behind these ordinances is a belated recognition of the beauty of the townhouse and of the need to establish zoning controls. Some of their benefit has been directed at those wishing to open a business and obtain a bank loan to invest in, refurbish, and preserve old homes. As a result, many machiya are being converted into shops and restaurants, assuring older residents that the appearance of their neighborhoods will remain intact and delighting passersby and visitors with the understated beauty of inner city architecture. However, businesses are not families, and the sense of community is still weakening, causing a number of organizations to emerge to encourage historic preservation.

The Kyoto Center for Community Collaboration (English website: http://machi.hitomachi-kyoto.jp/index_e.html) was founded in 1997 to develop a model plan for machiya renovation. In 2005, a generous benefactor helped initiate the Machiya Machizukuri Fund to allow collaboration with various specialists to counter some of the ongoing problems the townhouse owners continue to face.

In 2010, the World Monument Fund made possible the renovation of an old machiya in Kamanza-cho, a district once noted for its tea ceremony utensils crafted of iron. An old wooden house reconstructed under the guidance of architect Kinoshita Ryoichi is now open to the public. It is an excellent example of the simple beauty of traditional materials and centuries-old aesthetic principles. (The machiya, known as Kamanza-ya, is on the north side of Sanjo-dori, west of Sakaimachi-dori.)

MACHIYA CHARACTERISTICS

Five types of structures renovated into restaurants are mentioned in this book, but it is our examination of the machiya townhouse in particular that leads us to a fundamental understanding of the essential special elements in Japanese architecture.

TYPICAL MACHIYA FEATURES

The dark-wood lattice frontage of Kyoto townhouses is the most eye-catching feature of a traditional home. City residents prefer dark brown tints, whereas a red-stained *bengara* (Bengal red) lattice frontage is more often found in the countryside. The geometrical dimensions of the thin vertical slats may differ slightly from home to home, but their practicality in emitting light and giving residents a semblance of privacy makes them an enduring feature. Patterns vary too, but some denote specific enterprises, such as the pattern *itoya-goshi* used by a thread shop—*ito* meaning "thread," *ya* "shop," and *goshi* "lattice"—or the pattern *komeya-goshi* used by a rice (*kome*) shop. (The thread shop lattice was finer and farther spaced, admitting more light for the dyer to better distinguish color and needlework. Rice was equated with money and wealth, so a rice shop lattice was thicker and stronger to discourage thieves.)

Another defining feature of Japanese homes is their tiled roofs. The most popular pattern is *ichimonji*, an overlapping tile that creates a wave-like pattern on the roof: the eave tiles form a single slightly curved line resembling written calligraphy for *ichi* ("one"). Roof tiles are dense and high fired, made from clay found throughout Japan with different grades of lightness and porosity. Unglazed, the tile fires to a dark gray. (Recently, glass tiles are being produced as skylights to brighten dark interiors.)

With the exception of tea houses (*chaya*), which are places of entertainment, and the estates of aristocrats where two-story construction was permitted, most city dwellings were one story or one-and-a-half story (*chu-nikai*). Under the houses' eaves, vertical bars of clay *mushiko-mado* ("insect cage windows") allowed air to cir-

The entrance to the restaurant Les Trois Maisons.

culate in the crawl space above a suspended ceiling where goods might be stored or even a servant housed. Besides ventilation, one popular reason given for this feature is the belief that merchants might be able to use it to "look down on" passing warriors from above, something strictly forbidden in a hierarchical feudal society.

The curved lattice bamboo slats called *inuyarai* that extend from the front of some houses are said to protect the frontage from being marked by dogs or, if a corner home, to protect against the damage a wheeled cart would make turning the corner. Architectural restraints were dictated by ordinance, so this decorative touch is usually not found in the houses of commoners but in the homes of the wealthy and in *chaya*.

Occasionally, one spies the figure of the legendary demon-queller Shoki-san. This bewhiskered Chinese Taoist scholar healed a Tang-dynasty emperor by driving away the devil, thereby becoming an immortal clay fixture mounted on the eaves of Japanese homes, sword raised to protect residents from ill fortune.

Entrance to a townhouse is through one or two sliding doors that face the street, admitting guests and customers to an area that is on the ground level. The richer merchants often had elaborate roof-tiled gates, again with sliding lattice doors. Sometimes one can find a small doorway (*kuguri-do*) within a larger sliding door (*o-do*), under which one must stoop to enter. This entry was for family members or deliveries; the full-sized sliding doors were reserved for special occasions and guests.

In bigger homes, rectangular-shaped flat stonework (*ishi-tatami*) form the footpath to the entrance and extend to the "back" house. This passageway is left uncovered to allow rain to nourish the plants and bushes along the walk.

All houses are raised. Main pillars rest on stones inset in the earth, a sensible feature in an earthquake-prone land with a humid climate. Even when commoners' houses had earthen floors for the kitchen, a raised area was provided for eating and sleeping to avoid the dampness of Japan's cold winter and the moisture of the rainy season.

Eventually, interior rooms throughout the house all had tatami flooring, woven-reed mats of uniform measurement. These mats often became infested with insects, so it was (and still is) the practice in some neighborhoods to remove them and set them outside in the late summer sun to air, a troublesome task. This is another reason for the decline of tatami mats and the increased use of wooden floors, some heated. Today, various sprays and insect-resistant materials keep the intruders at bay, enabling homeowners to retain at least one tatami room for guests or as a temporary storage space.

Sliding doors between the rooms do not reach the suspended ceiling but are set within a grooved framework that holds the doors in place. Between the framework and ceiling are transoms (*ranma*), some of very simple yet elegant design. Usually carved of wood, these decorative transoms along with the *tokonoma* alcoves and garden materials reveal the aesthetic sense and financial status of the family.

One of the most desired features of a home is an area for a garden. Space will be made even if it is but a square meter in size, large enough only for a rock and a lone plant. Larger homes have an interior garden (*tsubo-niwa*) toward the front of the house, allowing light in and air to circulate. *Tsubo* means "pot" and *niwa*, "garden," suggesting a very simple arrangement of perhaps a single lantern, a bit of moss, and a few plants or a solitary tree. The inner garden (*naka-no-niwa*) is the largest and most elaborate in the house. It separated the front and back houses, adding privacy and again providing air and light. (Although it contains the word for "garden," the *tori-niwa*, another architectural feature, is actually an inner passageway, often passing through the dismally narrow kitchen. Charcoal and wood were used for cooking, and the high ceiling allowed smoke to dissipate upward, the drafty space carrying it away from the house interior. Skylights were usually found in the *tori-niwa* to give this area a bit of light, but traditional Japanese kitchens were never cozy gathering places.)

The Japanese bath and toilet were found outside the house proper, sometimes connected by a covered walk and not too far from street access so sewage could be removed. Today, most of the older squat toilets have been replaced with very high-tech models of Western-style toilets, a nod to the keenly hygienic people of Japan and its aging population.

Street-facing rooms were for business (*mise-no-ma*), and the back rooms were the family's living quarters. All the rooms had

The entrance to the restaurant Le Vieux Logis.

shoji doors (wood-framed rice-paper-covered doors) that faced the outside corridors. The rice paper was customarily changed at the New Year, but curious fingers might make temporary repair jobs necessary, especially with children in the house. The softened light that comes through the rice paper is the quintessential aesthetic element of interior ambience, softening the light by bestowing a subtle glow to the room's decorative features. Inner rooms are separated by *fusuma*, wood-framed sliding doors covered with a heavier single sheet of thick paper that is patterned and colored. In summer, the *fusuma* doors are changed into reed ones to admit breezes and convey a sense of coolness.

Some of the more elegant homes have snow-viewing doors (*yukimi-shoji*); the lower half is glass covered by a sliding paper panel that can be raised up to allow the residents—generally in a low posture while seated cross-legged on the floor—a glimpse of their snow-covered garden outside.

All homes, from those of ordinary people to aristocrats, had from one to several decorative alcoves (*tokonoma*) in rooms where they entertained or the family gathered. The simplest *tokonoma* might be a raised bit of flooring or a tatami mat with a vertical post of an exotic piece of wood and another partial post descending from the ceiling. In large homes, next to the *tokonoma,* another space was provided for a set of "staggered shelves" (*chigaidana*), some with tiny drawers or cabinets. The shape and type of wood used and the clay wall that backed the alcove were the result of special attention to detail.

The *tokonoma* alcove was where the family's treasured scrolls were hung and a flower arrangement placed. At the New Year, a pile of rice cakes topped with a strip of dried kelp and an orange were set out to welcome the gods. With the transformation to modern housing, especially in condominiums, this decorative detail has been greatly reduced, sacrificed to the need for more space and lessening the demand for hanging scrolls and flower arrangements. The demand for the decorative woods and workmanship needed to construct a *tokonoma* has also declined greatly, altering the nation's aesthetic consciousness. The *tokonoma* might be the one feature, along with tatami mat rooms, that has become rare in modern housing but is still seen in old Kyoto machiya.

MERCHANT HOUSES *(Shoka)*

Large homes used by rich merchants, *shoka*, appear as enlarged townhouses with much greater frontage as befitted their businesses. Taxes were determined by the width of the frontage; buildings behind and on alleys had lower taxes, something that is still true today. On a *shoka*'s property might be three gardens: *tsubo-niwa, naka-no-niwa,* and *oku-no-niwa* (small garden, inner garden, and back or rear garden). Large merchant compounds also had thick clay-walled storehouses (*kura*) to hold their stock and store seasonal furniture.

Examples of *shoka* restaurants listed in this book's dining guide are Ao and Katsukura.

STOREHOUSES *(Kura)*

Storehouses are usually distinctive square structures with straight, thick, white plaster and clay walls, dark tiled roofs, and small upper windows. The floor is raised, and the entrance is up a few steps that approach a thick, bank-vault-like door. The flame-resistant walls helped save the family's fortune of pottery, lacquerware, kimono, and scrolls when fire threatened. Under the tiled roof eaves the Chinese character for water (水) often appears, a reminder to the gods to spare the *kura* from the flames.

Small, high-placed windows admitted a little light, but otherwise the interior remained dark and cool.

Kura construction differs from prefecture to prefecture, and most have outer white plaster walls and thick wooden or metal doors with immense locks. Two of the most famous towns where this attractive architecture predominates are Kurashiki in Hyogo Prefecture and Omihachiman in Shiga Prefecture, both but a short distance from Kyoto.

In the southeastern part of Kyoto, ingenuity and a love of traditional architecture have yielded many charming restaurants in old sake breweries *(sakagura)* in Fushimi. These breweries are huge, thick, clay-walled and wooden structures with immense tiled roofs. The Gekkeikan sake brewery courtyard contains the source of its famed spirits—spring water in a stone-lined well—and a fine collection of huge wooden casks in which the mash used to ferment. This area of town has done much to renovate and restore some of its allure by restricting traffic and landscaping its waterways.

Examples of *kura* restaurants are Casa Bianca, Aoisho, Tsuki no Kurabito, and Shion, and those that use their adjacent *kura* for small parties are Robinson, Cameron, O-mo-ya Higashinotoin, Omo Café, and Chisoinaseya.

ESTATES AND VILLAS (*Yashiki*)

The earliest (11th–12th centuries) estates of the nobles in Japan were built in the *shinden* style (*shinden* means "sleeping hall"). A few of these estates were for very high-ranking nobles and situated on 120-square-meter blocks with the main residence facing south as well as ponds or streams surrounded by elaborate gardens. Most other estates were on smaller plots as befitted their owners' rank.

The low, one-story estate buildings had tile roofs and a verandah with a low railing that ran around the perimeter of the hall. All the rooms could be easily converted into the desired units by merely realigning the sliding *fusuma* doors that separated them. Entrance gates were on the eastern and western walls and were wide enough to admit carriages.

In the 15th and 16th centuries, the impact of the aesthetic values of the tea ceremony with its emphasis on elegant simplicity started to influence the villas being constructed by high-ranking samurai, wealthy merchants, and later, successful artists. A new type of construction called *sukiya* (literally, "refined abode") emerged. The villas of this period incorporated the understated look favored by tea ceremony enthusiasts but were based upon a modified layout of formal estates and featured a less formal interior and an asymmetry in design that reflected the tastes of the owners. The garden was essential, with views of it available from many rooms. Integrating the beauty of seasonal change into the residence was a concept that remains true even today even in the more cramped, inner city machiya.

The newly built Geihinkan, an official State Guest House in Kyoto's Imperial Park, is a modern example of an ancient layout. A high, reinforced concrete wall (made to resemble clay) surrounds the complex with a south-facing entrance. The inner building to the south is reserved for visitors of state and official functions such as dinners, receptions, and performances. The private quarters of the imperial family and their guests are connected by a low but elevated walkway that spans the garden to the sleeping quarters.

The Geihinkan garden is well appointed with a pond, a 3-meter-high waterfall, and an array of seasonal blooms that might inspire guests to pen a poetic sentiment. Unlike the inner gardens found in townhouses, this garden is expansive and surrounds the complex, bringing the seasons into immediate view.

Three villas converted into spacious restaurants are The Garden Oriental (Sodo Higashiyama), the former atelier of Takeuchi Seiho in the eastern hills; Ganko, the former estate of the Suminokura magnate on Kiyamachi-dori south of Nijo-dori; and Hakusan Sonso, the atelier and museum of the painter Hashimoto Kansetsu near Ginkaku-ji. (Hakusa Sonso is not listed in the restaurant guide but is worth a visit.)

TEAHOUSES *(Chaya)*

The Japanese word *chaya* literally means "teahouse," while *chashitsu* refers to a room where the tea ceremony is performed. *Chaya* are restaurants where *geiko* (the Kyoto term for *geisha*) and *maiko* (a *geiko* in training) entertain clients by playing traditional instruments, singing and dancing, and chatting pleasantly to clientele while keeping the sake flowing. The lyrical history of these formally indentured women—characterized by their great wit and talent and often unfortunate destinies—is with love songs and stories. The higher-ranking courtesans entertained high-ranking military lords and, increasingly, wealthy merchants who could afford to sponsor a beauty to aid them in their business ventures. Deals were secured and political plans hatched in some of the more famous *chaya*, and even

Detail of the exterior of the restaurant Ichi no Hunairi.

today politicians and businessmen entertain their constituents and clients in these places. However, wealth and status are not what they used to be, and the practice of keeping a *geiko* in hand-dyed kimono, gold-threaded woven *obi*, and exotic hairpins has become a thing of the past.

The most famous *geiko* and *maiko* districts in Kyoto are in Gion, Pontocho, and Miyagawacho, all located a bit north and south of Shijo-dori, near the Kamo River. Another district, Kamishichiken, is near Kitano Shrine in the northwest. As tastes in entertainment have changed, many of the lovely old *chaya* have been taken over by restaurateurs (some by former *geiko*) serving traditional cuisine to a regular clientele. (Most of the well-known *chaya* are only open at night, and their customers usually are regulars or those there by personal introduction.) Recently a number of these buildings have been converted into modern-style restaurants with table-and-chair seating and affordable lunch menus.

Historically, governmental and social dictates did not allow *chaya* construction to imitate the houses of the warrior class; instead, *chaya* followed the building codes for machiya townhouses. However, rather than being long and narrow with a house for the family in back of the business (*geiko* and *maiko* live and are trained in *okiya*, literally "storehouses"), the *chaya* is shallower, with entrances facing narrow streets and alleys. Many of the features of the *chaya* are similar to those of the *machiya*—raised tatami flooring and an inner garden and kitchen—but the *chaya* is composed of many small rooms and one or two larger rooms that can be easily altered to accommodate more customers by removing the sliding *fusuma* doors and doubling the space. Since these buildings were commercial entertainment establishments, each room comprises unique and interesting features in order to enhance the occasion by reflecting the sensual and poetic sensibilities of the performance: elaborate, delicate lattice work on paper doors, decorative gold leaf or paintings of an amorous nature on *fusuma* sliding doors, dropped ceilings employing unusual woodwork, alcoves displaying valued objects and a flower arrangement—beautiful settings that indulge the senses and inspire conversation.

Examples of *chaya* are Ichi no Hunairi, Baiwan Jukuairo, Korin, Karyo, Hanasaki in Gion, and Taotei.

FARMHOUSES *(Minka)*

I use the term *minka*—often translated as "farmhouse"—loosely. The word in fact has a much broader reference and literally means "houses of the people." Farmhouses (the proper term is *noka*) throughout Japan vary greatly, but I use the word *minka* here to mean thatched-roof dwellings with unrefined clay-and-mud walls constructed with huge timbers. Today, most thatched-roof houses in Japan remain outside city confines because of their flammability. Some of Japan's most famous farmhouses are in Gifu Prefecture at Shirakawa-go, a World Heritage Site. Some interiors have open earthen hearths where skewered fish could be slowly smoked over a slow-burning charcoal fire. The beauty of these houses lay in their rustic appeal, which was adopted by tea enthusiasts in the 14th century. This is the reason many estate tearooms and teahouses have thatched roofs and a small hearth for charcoal to heat the hanging kettle. The unadorned building materials embody the aesthetic concepts of *wabi* (rustic simplicity) and *sabi* (elegant simplicity).

Typically, the *minka* are huge, with no inner gardens but storage space for equipment and foodstuffs. The self-reliant farm family produced all their food and even clothing in many cases. Gardens, if they existed, were outside the main entrance.

There are few renovated farmhouses in Kyoto; two are the Kawaii Kanjiro Memorial Museum (which is not a restaurant) and the Azekura restaurant and grounds near Kamigamo Shrine.

BANKS OF THE MEIJI AND TAISHO ERAS

Over the centuries the Japanese have preferred an architecture of wood and never stone. This was so for various reasons: the constant threat of earthquakes is an obvious one; another may have been the difficulty of transporting large stones from quarry to town. There are, however, many stone mason shops in the city that market tombstones, and almost all old neighborhoods have stone images of the protective deity Jizo enclosed in small wooden shrines.

From ancient times, the soil in this volcanic archipelago gave up an abundant variety of rocks and stones, some so mag-

Detail of the stone archway entrance to the building Shinpuhkan.

nificent in size and shape they were incorporated into landscape gardens. Originally, these early garden rocks represented the five isles of the Taoist Immortals or were used to form bridges over manmade ponds. Zen gardens further developed the use of rocks, using them to depict rivers, the sea, and islands. But stones remained ornamental and were not used as construction material in Japan except as foundation stones.

During the Warring States Era (1467–1573), the country was plunged into a century of chaos. Destruction was all around. Regional rulers retreated to mountainous areas or built fortresses on flatlands commanding sweeping views. Although these castle keeps were built of wood with thick clay-and-plaster walls, the surrounding outer walls were often steep stone palisades formed from granite. Probably one of the most magnificent examples of castle masonry is in Kyushu, at Kumamoto Castle. In Kyoto, although Nijo Castle was mostly for administrative use, its stone walls set the compound well apart from the estates of the nobles and imperial court that had only tile-topped clay-and-plaster walls.

The Nijo Castle walls were not especially high, nor was the moat deep, but the psychological impact of the fortification was clear. (The sunken walk along the Horikawa river near Nijo Castle has a signboard explaining the diversity of stones gathered and contributed by Tokugawa subordinates. Stones from afar were transported by ship and then pulled over logs to reach their destination. All building was done by sheer manpower.)

During the Meiji (1868–1912) and Taisho (1912–26) periods, Japan opened its doors to the West and accelerated a process of westernization after centuries of isolation. Western fashion was quickly embraced by the emperor, who abandoned the kimono and sword and thereafter appeared wearing formal Western-style suits. Railroads, museums, post offices, banks, and universities modeled on their European counterparts were constructed, laying the foundation of Kyoto as a modern city. Like their Western counterparts, these edifices were constructed of stone, usually granite, and brick, and had thick walls, sturdy floors, and high ceilings.

Japan is rich in granite, with quarries found all over the country. The stone was an ideal choice for bank construction, as its subdued coloring evoked trust and safety with depositors. Cash was stored in vaults behind thick iron, later steel, doors. Bank interiors had tall leaded windowpanes, and their floors often featured attractive tile work or inset colored stone. The banks were substantial and represented Japan's entry into the international financial world. The famous names in banking—Sumitomo, Mitsui, Mitsubishi—still exist today. Smaller, private banks were also established to finance the tobacco or kimono trade, but these buildings have recently been absorbed and abandoned as houses of finance, and some have been artfully renovated. Their high ceilings and open spaces make them ideal as restaurants and wedding halls.

Examples of banks turned into restaurants are Flowing, Cara Ragazza, and Bon Bon Café. Several restaurants are in Taisho stone buildings: Due in the former American Center, Café Chocolat in the former Mainichi Newspaper Office, both on Sanjo-dori, and the various eateries in Shinpuhkan, once the headquarters of Nippon Telegraph and Telephone.

The Beauty of Machiya

PHOTOGRAPHS BY BEN SIMMONS

An old Kyoto shop still displaying its original mounted, carved wooden sign.

A fold-down battari-shogi *bench between two sliding lattice doors.*

A neighboring roof-tiled house casting its shadow against the frontage of a wooden- and earthen-walled house.

Various styles of lattice design highlighted by inner shoji *paper sliding doors.*

The vivid contrast of unstained and black-stained lattice frontage.

A fold-down battari-shogi *bench for displayings goods or seating guests.*

A lattice front bay window, occasionally used as a window display.

New inuyarai *bamboo fencing blending effortlessly with the soft hues of the cypress lattice frontage.*

The subtle hues of natural materials in traditional
architecture seduce and sooth the eye. For centuries in
Japan, such materials—cypress and cedar, bamboo and
stone surfaces, earthen walls and baked-clay tiled roofs, low
decorative rocks, potted plants—have created some of the
most refined façades in the world. The sparing use of color
and glitter emphasizes how carpenters, masons, plasterers,
and potters use understated skill to guide and inspire, to
blend function and beauty.

A poster announcing cherry blossom dances in the Gion district.

A signboard illustrating Kyoto vegetables and tidbits of skewered chicken.

A hand-painted face of Jizo in a neighborhood shrine.

A clay image of demon-queller Shoki-san, who protects households against misfortune.

A wavy line of roof tiles (ichimon-gawara) *outlining a* mushiko-mado *earthen window.*

An oval mushiko-mado *earthen window above a wall of wood-plank siding.*

Wave-like roof tiles (ichimongara) *against a symmetrical* mushiko-mado *plaster window.*

The pristine white plaster walls of a tiled roof shop with a cloud-shaped (kumo-gata) *window.*

Stone, plaster, earth, and wood were put to good use to guard against the whims of fire, serving a decorative as well as practical need. Thick-walled storehouses protect treasured items from conflagration; tile roofs, unlike thatch, protect against fire, while solid beams better withstand heat. Plaster and earthen windows with narrow openings keep out intruders and allow air to circulate during hot, humid summers. And joinery techniques resist the shifting caused by earthquakes.

A thick hinged window of a storehouse (kura) with roof-tiled eave and cloud-shaped window design.

ABOVE: *A plaster-walled storehouse (kura) with a red-stained lattice behind an onion-bulb-shaped (giboshi-gata) window.*
RIGHT: *A covered vertical-bar plaster window on a storehouse (kura).*

A kitchen well-wheel beside a mizuya *storage chest topped with earthen figures of Hotei, one of the Seven Lucky Gods.*

A stairway chest (kaidan-dansu) *used for storage as well as moving between floors.*

A bomb shelter converted into a wine cellar at the restaurant Ame du Garçon.

An inlaid stone corridor (tori–niwa) linking the front and back houses.

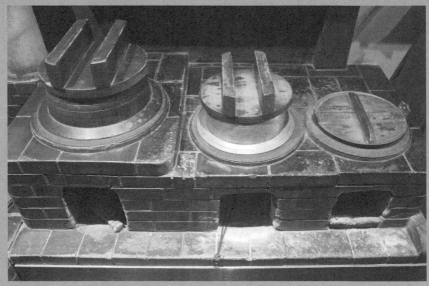

A tile-covered hearth with metal cooking pots and wooden lids.

With their soft, natural tones, the finely textured clay walls that cover interiors provide a backdrop for fine art. Thickly woven straw-colored rush mats (tatami) soften the underlying wooden-plank floors and complement the interior walls.

Earthen pots in a restaurant's entrance.

A scroll-backed flower arrangement in a restaurant entrance.

A flower arrangement before a scroll in a restaurant's alcove (tokonoma).

Elaborate joinery of exposed beams offset by white plastered walls.

A transom (ranma) with a flower motif between rooms with suspended ceilings in the renovated townhouse Kamanzaya.

Exposed beams in the entrance to a weaving company.

Ceilings are suspended planks of wood that can range from exotic and expensive to pragmatically simple. Thick paper sliding doors (*fusuma*) end short of the ceiling, leaving space for transoms (*ranma*) that let light and air circulate. *Ranma* reflect individual tastes and regional differences, with Kyotoites favoring delicately carved scenes and simple floral patterns—many with poetic or seasonal themes.

A convex converted bathroom ceiling, designed to allow steam to run down its slanted sides.

A tatami tearoom with an inset section for a hearth in the renovated townhouse Kamanzaya.

Vertical "snow-viewing" (yukimi) wooden lattice and paper shoji doors.

The view of the inner garden in the renovated townhouse Kamanzaya.

Enclosed raked gravel area of an inner garden. Two store-houses (kura) are part of this merchant's estate.

Townhouses are long and narrow with shared walls and dark interiors. Skylights are essential for light and air. Larger properties feature compact gardens near the street entrance, often with a stone lantern, large rock, and a few plants. An inner garden provides an elaborate space with seasonal flowering bushes and trees, treating inhabitants to a year-round display of blooms or foliage. Water basins add glistening stone surfaces, covered with jewel-green moss.

An inner garden viewed from beneath woven-reed sudare *blinds.*

The skillful arrangement of stones and a water basin in an inner garden.

A moss-covered tsukubai
water basin in an inner garden,
designed to produce the soothing
sound of running water.

A stone lantern in the inner garden of a restaurant.

A water basin in the inner garden of the renovated townhouse Kamanzaya, with a groundcover of fern and azalea.

First-floor dining in O-mo-ya Higashinotoin.

Second floor dining in O-mo-ya Higashinotoin, with a view of a pine tree in the inner garden beyond woven-reed sudare *blinds.*

The chef of Takara in his renovated townhouse restaurant in the Nishijin district.

The chef of Kurosuke, a renovated teahouse (chaya) *in the Kamishichiken geiko district.*

Japan's cuisine reflects and complements the subtlety of its architectural tradition: an artfully arranged assembly of natural ingredients with minimal flavoring. Restaurants in machiya are inevitably small in size, but many feature gardens and natural lighting that assure diners of a traditionally comfortable atmosphere.

Restaurant
Guide

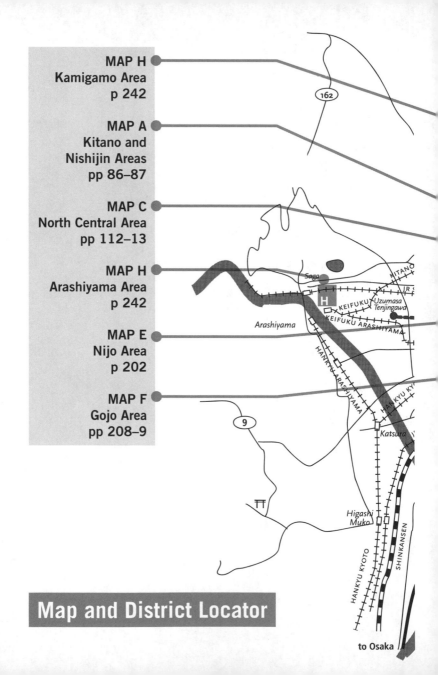

162

KITANO

JR S

Saga

H

KEIFUKU *Uzumasa Tenjingawa*

Arashiyama KEIFUKU ARASHIYAMA

HANKYU ARASHIYAMA

HANKYU KY

9

Katsura

Higashi Muko

HANKYU KYOTO

SHINKANSEN

Map and District Locator

to Osaka

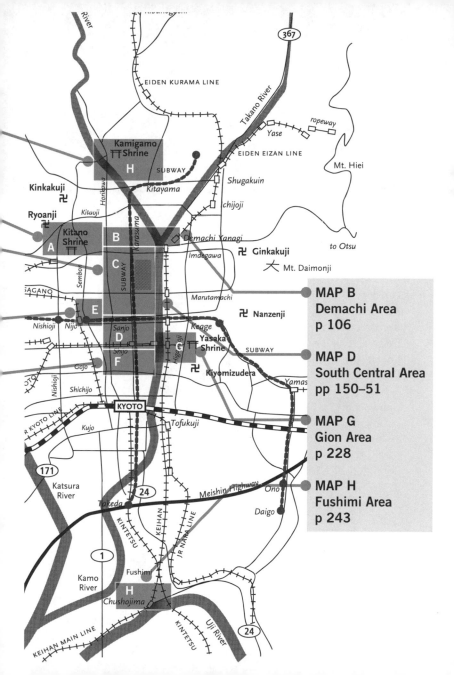

MAP B
Demachi Area
p 106

MAP D
South Central Area
pp 150–51

MAP G
Gion Area
p 228

MAP H
Fushimi Area
p 243

ANRI DI SPAGHETTI スパゲッティアンリ

Italian   A1

A red awning spans this old shop with its diagonal frontage, a construction technique used to provide better visibility to traffic on narrow streets. The dark wooden sliding doors have panels of frosted glass, and the exterior walls are white plaster. The interior seats only 12 in what used to be the shop area, now an Italian restaurant. The owners live upstairs. Pink paisley wall paper gives the tiny, comfortable setting a fresh glow.

A pasta lunch with a small salad and coffee or tea is around ¥1,000.

➡ East side of Omiya-dori, 2 blocks north of Kitaoji-dori. 🕐 11am–5pm (LO 2:30pm)/6pm–10pm (LO 9:30pm). Closed Monday and 1st Sunday of month. 📞 075-491-2447. @ www.spaghetti-anri.com. 🏠 北区紫野下門町５２番地３

CAFÉ FROSCH カフェフロシュ

Café · A8

The *chu-nikai* (one-and-a-half-story old house) once belonged to one of the Nishijin district's famous kimono weavers. Even today, the sound of nearby looms provides a syncopated background as you stroll the neighborhood.

The front lattice doors have been replaced with glass doors, which are removed during fair weather. Patrons may wear shoes, except in the raised middle section with its tatami flooring. Exposed beams and skylights extend upward in the back room, with light also coming in from the small back garden, making the atmosphere inviting and casual.

The menu is unique with an all-you-can-eat brunch on weekends for a mere ¥1,500. Beverages are ¥200 extra. Other days feature a daily lunch, sandwiches, and cake sets. Home-baked bread and bagels are available at the register.

➡ East side of Shichihonmatsu-dori, 2 blocks north of Imadegawa-dori, opposite small park. 🕐 Weekdays: 11am–6pm. Weekend brunch: 10:30am–3pm. 📞 075-205-2703. @ www.cafe-frosch.com. 🏠 上京区七本松通り五辻上ル

CAFÉ HAKUYA 箔屋

Café · A5

The gold and silver foil threads for *obi* that belt traditional kimono (*haku*) used to be prepared in this two-story building. A finely renovated façade with the calligraphy for *hakuya* marks the entrance.

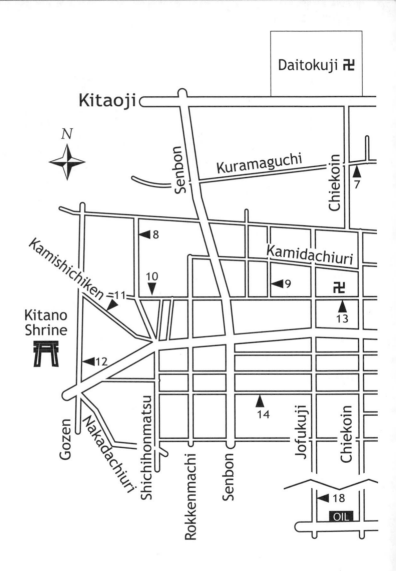

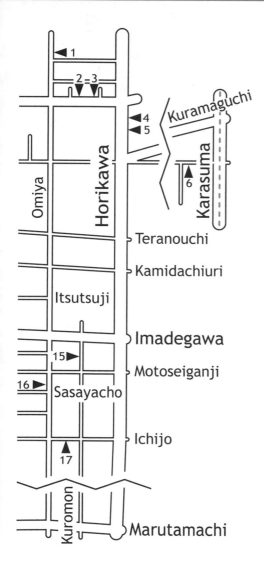

A1 Anri di Spaghetti
A2 Yubanzai Komameya
A3 Hatsuneya
A4 Shibuya
A5 Café Hakuya
A6 Prangipani
A7 Sarasa Nishijin
A8 Café Frosch
A9 Les Trois Maisons
A10 Vertigo
A11 Kurosuke
A12 Shion
A13 Toriiwa-ro
A14 Oedo
A15 Meirin
A16 Takara
A17 Le Vieux Logis
A18 Ryokiden

The café sits within Nishijin, the weaving and dyeing district of Kyoto. Many private ateliers still prepare thread for the looms, which provide the same rhythmic background clacking that has been heard for centuries. The present owner's

father-in-law worked in the west-facing room with his materials spread before him, winding fine sheets of foil around individual silk threads. This old workroom has been converted to a dining area with a table and chairs and a few potted plants. Further back, what were once tatami rooms have been updated with a wooden floor and, in front of the kitchen area, a new counter, which features an elaborate *kamidana*. This kitchen-god shelf is often found in older homes and, in accordance with Shinto tradition, an unpainted wooden tray typically holds offerings of rice, sake, or a cake, along with a simple white ceramic vase filled with a branch of *sakaki*, the greenery sacred to Shinto. The back area, once the site of the storehouse, has been cleared and made into a garden.

The menu has two items: a vegetable curry for ¥800 and a hamburger set for ¥900, with a beverage for ¥200 extra. Cakes are made on the premises, so just ask what is available.

➡ East side of Horikawa-dori, just south of Kitaoji-dori. 🕐 11am–6pm (LO 5:30pm). Closed Sunday and Monday. 📞 075-411-1218. 🚗 北区堀川通り北大路下ル東側

HATSUNEYA 初音屋

Noodles   A3

This shop takes its name from a nearby neighborhood, Hatsune ("the first sound"). The dark lattice front is set off with a dark green door. You move through two wooden-floor rooms with cushion seating and into a large open area with table-and-chair seating for 30.

Large exposed beams overhead and natural clay walls add a handsome touch and almost match the color of the *soba* served here.

Some *soba* shops use 100% buckwheat, which tends to crumble and is hard to eat with chopsticks. The flour used here is from Hokkaido and is an 80/20 mixture of *soba* and wheat. This blend is tasty and full flavored. A small well-maintained garden brings in soft northern light.

Bowls of *soba* start around ¥800.

➡ North side of Kitaoji-dori, between Horikawa-dori and Omiya-dori. 🕐 11:30am–2:30pm/5:30pm–10pm. Closed Thursday. 📞 075-492-9191. @ www.soba-hatsuneya.com. 🏠 北区紫野西御所田町2 3

KUROSUKE くろすけ

Japanese   A11

Kurosuke resides in Kyoto's oldest *geiko* district, Kamishichiken—meaning "seven teahouses to the north." The seven teahouses were built for warlord Hideyoshi Toyotomi as part of his plan for an extravagant public tea party at the Kitano Tenman Shrine in 1589. Earlier, in 1444, a terrific fire had destroyed the shrine, but many pieces of valuable timber were saved. There was enough wood, so the legend goes, to construct the seven *chaya*. The

remaining salvages of the shrine lend a lustrous quality to the buildings' frontages and interiors and are part of what makes this entertainment district so alluring and refined.

Kurosuke is identifiable by a hanging *noren* curtain that announces when it is open and by a Meiji-style lantern mounted on the lower eaves.

The entrance, where shoes are left, has a ceiling that soars upward to a skylight and an old stone well covered with a bamboo top. Above the well are red and white fans inscribed with the names of the *maiko* (apprentice *geiko*) who patronize the *chaya*.

Counter seating is available on the first floor, but most customers ascend a stepped chest (the *kaidan-dansu*, one of Japan's unique furniture items, doubles as a storage chest and stairway) to reach the second floor with tatami seating. Private parties and small groups can make their way along a covered passageway to a separate building hidden from street view. Between the buildings is a beautifully landscaped inner garden designed to delight viewers with its year-round blooms.

The standing screen at the top of the stairs pictures two courtesans created in battledore style, a quilting technique in which stuffed textiles are attached directly onto a hard surface—in this case, a screen. The posts throughout the building are of exotic and expensive wood, a testimony to the value Japanese place on natural materials in design.

The fence-like enclosure around the downstairs register is where abacus-handy accountants once settled bills. The very handsome *mizuya* (wooden cupboards where dishes are stored in traditional old homes) glisten from frequent polishing. Their size and sturdiness indicate a well-established, successful business.

The lunch *bento* at ¥3,150 offers several versions of the bean curd made daily at the nearby famous Toyoke tofu shop, but vegetable and fish dishes also form a generous portion of this restaurant's fine cuisine.

➡️ North side of diagonal street running northwest from Imadegawa-dori and Shichihonmatsu-dori intersection to east gate of Kitano Tenmangu Shrine. 🕐 11:30am–2:30pm (LO)/5pm–9:30pm (LO). Closed Tuesday. 📞 075-466-4889. 🔴rsvp Recommended. @ www.kurochiku.co.jp. 🚗 上京区今出川通り七本松西入ル

LE VIEUX LOGIS ルブユーロジ

French   A17

At the entrance of the picturesque narrow approach to Le Vieux Logis is a gate with a sign that says, "Yokoso," the slogan of Japan's campaign to welcome tourists.

The restaurateur, Pascal Soyer, moved to this quiet location and redid a 120-year-old weaver's house where he could practice his culinary art. Table-and-chair seating can accommodate 14 customers. Lunch is ¥1,800 for an appetizer, main dish, dessert, and coffee; dinner is from ¥3,600.

➡️ South side of Ichijo-dori, 2 blocks west of Horikawa-dori. 🕐 11:30am–2:30pm (LO 2pm)/5:30pm–9:30pm (LO 9pm). Closed Monday. 📞 075-411-8236. @ www.kyotolevieuxlogis.com. 🚗 上京区一条道堀川道り西入ル

LES TROIS MAISONS レ トロワ メゾン

Tucked away on one of Kyoto's numerous no-name streets in the weaving and dyeing district is this 140-year-old two-story townhouse, which has been transformed into a café and *auberge* offering vernight accommodation.

To the north of Les Trois Maisons are two former weaving companies, now designated cultural properties of Kyoto City. On a nearby corner, a wooden sign marks the Itsutsuji-dono, the site of a "cloister government" palace that existed here in the 13th century. Built in 1203, it was the residence of the retired emperor Gotoba.

The building housing Les Trois Maisons originally belonged to a family in the kimono business. The offices were in the front room, and special customers and guests were received in the back room facing the spacious garden. Having undergone minimal renovations, the building has kept its traditional ambience, but heating and air-conditioning make the restaurant comfortable and casual to dine in.

Inside, exposed beams support the ceiling and a second-story window provides a soft, soothing light. All rooms look onto the garden, and a smaller platform with cushion seating overlooks the garden further back. The *tori-niwa* passageway to the back gallery passes an old well and is covered with gravel and steppingstones.

The loom rooms in the back of the property have been turned into an art gallery. Even today, these back rooms are warm and humid in summer and damp and cold in winter—ideal conditions to weave silk threads' flexibility. Skylights provided light by which dyes were shown to their most natural advantage. Looms were tall and, before the Jacquard loom became commonplace, worked by two people—one standing to raise and lower the warp thread and one seated weaver who passed the shuttle with the weft back and forth.

The second floor has been converted into an inn with rooms that advertise soft, deep mattresses ensuring a good night's rest. Rooms are about ¥12,000 per person per night with no meals included.

The menu is in French and English, and lunch is around ¥1,100, with a choice of desserts made on the premises.

➡ East side of unnamed street, just north of Itsutsuji-dori, 2 blocks east of Senbon-dori. 🕐 Noon–9pm. 📞 075-950-7299. @ www.ctn139.com. 🚗 上京区千本通 り 五辻東入ル2筋目上ル

MEIRIN 美鈴

Chinese A15

In one of Kyoto's ubiquitous small alleys, a *noren* curtain, simple lattice frontage, and a low table with restaurant name cards help identify Meirin, now one of the area's favorite restaurants, offering Chinese food, but in individual Japanese-like servings.

On the first floor, two tables snugly seat 4 people each and a narrow counter another 4, an indication of the very small size of many of the houses in this weaving and dyeing district. Upstairs is a tatami room with two low tables. Both floors have a simple *tokonoma*; the one on the first floor features a Chinese scroll.

Lunch, however, is full size and well worth the price, consisting of three dishes and a dessert and Chinese tea for ¥1,000. Boxes with chopsticks and wooden spoons (for dessert) are placed on each table, a pleasant departure from the use of disposable chopsticks in many other eateries. The menu changes with the season.

➡ West side of Kuromon-dori, just south of Imadegawa-dori, 1 block east of Omiya-dori. 🕐 11:30am–2pm/5:30pm–9pm. Closed Monday. 📞 075-441-7597. rsvp Recommended. 🚗 上京区黒門通り元誓願寺上ル寺今町511

OEDO 大江戸

Japanese   A14

Originally comprising two buildings, Oedo was renovated in 1996 and is now identified by a poured concrete wall, not a lattice front. While the outer structure has been completely modernized, the interior retains its 100-year-old beams.

The street-front house was demolished and replaced with a very large rectangular pond stocked with beautiful tri-colored Nishiki koi. The two-story back house was rebuilt with a raised tatami seating area that overlooks the koi pond. Attractive wooden tables and chairs and a counter area provide seating for about 30.

Oedo is one of the best places to sample the Japanese dish *tonkatsu*—breaded deep-fried pork. The ¥1,450 mini *tonkatsu* dish presents medallions of succulent pork, still pink within (pork products in Japan are highly regulated and safe), with a mound of shredded cab-

bage, a small slice of pineapple, and red miso soup. A container with
rice is placed on the table for customers to help themselves.

➡️ South side of Sasayacho-dori, just east of Senbon-dori. 🕐 11:30am–2pm/5pm–
9pm. Closed Monday and 3rd Tuesday of month. 📞 075-441-2022. 🚗 上京区笹屋
町通千本東入南側

PRANGIPANI フランジパニ

Café   A6

The location of this
spacious 80-year-old
house, a few meters back
from Kuramaguchi-dori,
buffers the sound and
sight of passing cars and
allows plenty of light
to enter the glass front.
Several tables seat about
20; in back the raised
tatami room has been retained with its formal *tokonoma*. Checkered
shoji paper doors filter the light coming in from the garden, providing a
uniquely lit backdrop, and large leafy potted plants give the café a fresh
feeling.

When asked why the name is spelled "prangipani" and not
"frangipani," the proprietress says that's the way the flower is spelled in
Indonesian.

A simple café menu is in Japanese, and the chalkboard outside lists
lunch, often "spicy chicken curry," which is ¥650 with ¥200 extra for
coffee.

The atmosphere is casual and spacious enough to allow you to
sit back and read, something three out of the five patrons were doing
when I was there.

➡️ 1 block south of Kuramaguchi-dori, just west of Karasuma-dori. 🕐 10:00am–7pm. Closed Sunday. 📞 075-411-2245. 🚗 上京区室町通り鞍馬口下ル森之木町 462

RYOKIDEN 綾綺殿

Café   A18

Ryokiden's building once belonged to a rice dealer and is now owned by the 200-year-old Yamanaka Oil shop around the corner on Shimodachi-uri-dori, an unmistakable landmark with a giant waterwheel in front.

The year 2008 was the 1,000-year anniversary of the literary classic *The Tale of Genji;* to celebrate, the city marked sites corresponding to those known at the time the work was written. Ryokiden is one of these. On its wall is a map of the old Heian capital in the vicinity. Scholars speculate that here was the site of the musician's quarters—Ryokiden—pictured next to the map.

There is chair seating in the front and back, kitchen, and bar in the center of the café. A brick cooking unit in the back of the shop represents a "modern" version of the rounded clay ovens used in country homes. The cast iron wood-heated bathtub outside was typical of many early 20th-century homes where the bath and toilet were separate from the house. Fortunately, the present facility is state-of-the art (press the top of the unit on the wall to flush).

The suspended ceiling was taken down in the back room, exposing the beams and lightening up the dark wooden interior. The bench seating along the wall shows the height of the former tatami room, and attractive glass doors give a view of the tiny garden.

Seemingly at odds with the weighty history enveloping the narrow streets here, Ryokiden serves three kinds of panini for ¥650: vegetable; eggplant and anchovy; and tuna. Any drink ordered with the meal is ¥50 yen off; the beverage list includes black tea and herb tea and freshly ground Italian Morgami coffee. Belgian waffles, tiramisu, and chiffon cake are also on the menu. The non-English menu's photos make ordering easy.

➡ East side of Jofukuji-dori, just north of Shimodachiuri-dori. 🕐 10am–6pm. Closed Wednesday. 📞 075-801-3125. @ www.ryokiden.com. 🚗 上京区浄福寺通り下立売上ル

SARASA NISHIJIN さらさ西陣

Café   **A7**

This might be one of the most unique eateries in Kyoto: an 80-year-old bathhouse with kaleidoscope-like tilework on the walls. I actually remember bathing here. It was small but charming, with one large bath on each side of the dividing wall and hot-and-cold water faucets along the other walls.

The café is on two levels: one comprises the entrance where the receptionist sat and the rooms where people changed their clothes; the other was once the bathing area, elevated to accommodate the deep bathtubs. A mixed collection of tables and chairs provides seating for about 30 people.

The building's façade has a small, curving gable-roof extending over the entrance, an elegant architectural feature that was a clear sign of wealth and workmanship.

The café is set back from the road a few meters to allow patrons to park their bicycles. The fare is simple pasta or rice dishes. Lunch is about ¥1,000; coffee or tea and cake sets are another popular choice.

➡ South side of Kuramaguchi-dori, just east of Chiekoin-dori. 🕐 Noon–10pm. Closed Wednesday. 📞 075-432-5075. @ sarasan2.exblog.jp. 🚗 北区紫野東藤ノ森町11-1

SHIBUYA 渋谷

French — A4

A menu mounted on a stand is outside the two-storied tiled-roof building, whose elegant, traditional black and white exterior sets expectations for the finely prepared French cuisine within. Downstairs has seating for 6 at the counter and

for 4 at tables in a raised section, a reminder of the tatami area that was formerly a part of this 80-year-old shop. Upstairs is table-and-chair seating for 10. The exposed interior posts against the white plaster walls make a refreshing background for the beautifully presented dishes, many of which include Kyoto vegetables (*kyo-yasai*) in season.

The "A course" lunch for ¥2,100 started with fresh salmon over lightly pickled vegetables, followed by mountain-potato (*yamaimo*) soup, home-baked bread, green salad, and a main course of white fish with grilled vegetables, ending with dessert and coffee or tea.

➡ East side of Horikawa-dori, just south of Kitaoji-dori. ⏱ Noon–2pm/6pm–9pm. Closed Tuesday. 📞 075-411-2332. @ www.kitaooji-shibuya.com. 🚗 北区堀川北大路下ル東側

SHION 四恩

Japanese   A12

Though located in the environs of a shrine, Shion's imposing three-story, white-walled storehouse (*kura*) imparts a different kind of atmosphere. *Kura* in the compounds of private homes contain family treasures,

but this one belonged to a sake-making brewery. As with all *kura,* the walls are thick white plaster to shield the interior from flames, and the windows are small to keep the inside dark and the temperature even.

The 80-year-old *kura* has a spacious interior: dark-stained overhead beams rise two stories above the table-and-chair seating for 30. The original packed-earth floor has been covered with cut stone and a raised tatami section. A counter with seating for 6 is farther back. All noodles are produced in-house, and instead of the usual thick and square-cut servings, Shion's are slender and rounded.

Shion also operates as a café between dining times. An outside menu and photos at the entrance show the set courses, all of which include either homemade buckwheat or wheat noodles, the house specialty. The ¥1,200 Kyoto course of noodles comes with a small selection of homemade vegetables and pickles and a bowl of rice. Dessert is a scoop of green-tea ice cream and a cup of hot tea. Dinner courses start at ¥2,300.

➡️ East side of Gozen-dori, just north of Imadegawa-dori, directly east of Kitano Tenmangu Shrine. 🕐 11am–9pm. Closed Wednesday. 📞 075-463-0451. @ www.s-1.mc/shion. 🚗 上京区馬喰町８９７

TAKARA 多伽羅

Japanese/American   A16

This lovely 100-year-old structure has been renovated again (it was formerly known as Focal Point) and made more spacious. And it has introduced nouvelle cuisine to the Nishijin district.

The young chef, Dan Tominaga, was partly raised in New York City and has returned to Japan to try his hand at a blend of cooking styles and modern dishes in a very traditional old townhouse.

All seating is at tables. The house is divided into two parts. An inner garden lets in plenty of light in addition to the glass-tile sky-lights. The front room has been redone in light-colored wood, lightening up a formerly shadowy space. High, thick beams crisscross the white plastered ceiling in the back room, making the interior spacious yet cozy. A stairway leads to a sliver of a second floor with three small tables and a bit of privacy and a wonderful view of the first floor and garden.

The soup-and-salad lunch is ¥1,500 and the very filling hamburger lunch with delicately sliced French fries is ¥1,800. The Japanese boxed lunch is ¥3,000.

West side of Omiya-dori, 2 blocks south of Imadegawa-dori. ⏰ 11:30am–1:30pm (LO)/5:30pm–8:30pm (LO). Closed Sunday and 3rd Monday of month. 📞 075-417-0885. 🚃 上京区大宮通元誓願寺下ル

TORIIWA-RO 鳥岩楼

Japanese   A13

This building was moved here from the Gion district about 40 years ago. With its highly decorated stone-path approach and hanging red "umbrella" signifying a prosperous business, the entrance has a fussy feel. There are so many fine objects, one realizes this is not Zen-inspired minimalist Japan. Originally the residence of a tea ceremony aficionado, the 80-year-old Taisho-era house is a beautiful example of the "retro" taste that prevailed during the '20s and '30s in Japan. From the folded-umbrella stone lantern in the entrance to the multitude of different ceilings upstairs, staggered shelves in the alcove, intricate lattice windows, and gold-foil-backed sliding paper doors, the building abounds in quaint yet sophisticated architectural detail.

One transom on the second floor is of two rice spatulas, another is in the shape of Mt. Hiei. The 60-year-old marble tables are so low on the tatami floor that they are more like trays. The inner garden is dense with two tall stone lanterns, an arched stone bridge, and lots of greenery. Delicate railings enclose the upstairs veranda, where paper sliding *shoji* doors are mostly in the *yukimi* ("snow viewing") style, with one papered panel that can be raised to both let in light as well as view the snow outside. Other sliding paper panels are at floor level to allow a cool cross breeze to enter, a very necessary feature in Kyoto's pre-airconditioned, hot and humid summers.

This restaurant is famous for its *mizutori*, a chicken hotpot, but at lunchtime, only *oyaku-donburi*, a chicken and egg sauce topping on a bowl of rice with a small cup of chicken broth, is served for ¥800. This is a very reasonable price to pay to enter and enjoy this marvelous architectural timepiece. Dinner is ¥6,000.

➡️ South side of Itsutsuji-dori, 1 block north of Imadegawa-dori, just west of Chiekoin-dori (across from small temple Honryu-ji). 🕐 Lunch: noon–2pm. Dinner: 5pm–8:30pm. Closed Thursday. 📞 075-441-4004. @ www3.ocn.ne.jp/~mao_utty/toriiwa. 🚌 上京区五辻通智恵光院西入ル

VERTIGO ヴァーデイゴ

Italian   A10

This solid, two-story building features a glassed-in (open in summer) frontage and a rose-colored banner with its name on it instead of a *noren* curtain.

The 80-year-old weaving studio has been handsomely converted.

The central suspended ceiling was removed, exposing the high interior beams, and a back garden with tables and chairs was placed outside for summer dining. The restaurant thus has a spacious, open feel without sacrificing its distinctly traditional setting. The exterior walls have been replastered and the interior ones redone in earthen colors that set off the beauty of the dark-stained woodwork. A bar with counter seating accommodates 4. The small kitchen is now glass enclosed. One typical area for storing kitchen utensils (*mizuya*) forms part of the wall in the front room.

The restaurant's owner is a fan of the Hitchcock movie *Vertigo*, hence the name, which has nothing to do with the effect of the wine imbibed.

Many of the smaller streets in Kyoto have no names and are identified instead by *cho* or district. On hundreds of old houses in Kyoto, including Vertigo, you will see an address marker made of a long narrow strip of tin. It is in fact an advertisement for Jintan, a brand of breath freshener. After Japan won the Russo-Japanese War in 1905, Jintan appropriated the motif of the Japanese soldier—whose Western-style uniform was modeled on that worn by the German politician Otto von Bismarck (1815–98)—to represent an envoy of medicine and used it on address signs throughout the cities of Kyoto, Osaka, Nagoya, and Tokyo. In 2010, Jintan contributed more signs to Kyoto, inviting different calligraphers to write the addresses. Today, there are about 800 Jintan signs in the city.

Vertigo serves three lunches: pasta with salad from ¥1,050; pizza and salad for ¥1,200; and hamburger with soup and salad for ¥1,880. All lunches include coffee or tea. A selection of desserts is available during the afternoon. Lunch is generally from ¥1,000, dinner from ¥3,000.

➡ North side of Itsutsuji-dori, just east of Shichihonmatsu-dori. 🕐 11:30am–10pm (LO 9:30pm). Closed Tuesday. 📞 075-461-1056. 🚌 上京区五辻道七本松東入ル北側

YUBANZAI KOMAMEYA ゆばんざいこ豆や

Japanese   A2

This 80-year-old residence was remodeled as a restaurant specializing in *yuba*, thin sheets of skimmed soya "milk." *Yuba* is primarily a Kyoto specialty because of all the Zen temples in the city and is often served in place of raw fish. The entrance is to the left of a case from which tofu desserts and tofu soft cream are displayed and sold.

The stone entrance leads to a dark wooden interior; counter and table-and-chair seating downstairs and floor seating in the loft-like upstairs hold about 30 customers. The ceiling is crisscrossed with large exposed beams, giving the restaurant a rustic atmosphere.

The hearty fare, all tofu based, is a boon to vegetarians. Lunch starts at ¥1,700 and consists of about six dishes using soya products: marinated; deep-fried; soya flakes on a salad; fresh *yuba*; soup; and a bowl of rice with a ginger topping. This is very filling, a delightful find for vegetarians and tofu enthusiasts alike.

➡ North side of Kitaoji-dori, between Horikawa-dori and Omiya-dori. 🕐 11:30am–2:30pm/5:30pm–10pm. Closed Wednesday. 📞 075-495-8800. @ www.ueda-yuba.co.jp. 🚗 北区紫野西御所田町23

AOISHO 葵匠

Japanese   B2

The 140-year-old pickle shop Tanabeso is a well-known shop in the Demachiyanagi shopping district. Most of the pickles in Kyoto come from vegetables grown in the northern outskirts of the city. Especially for farmers in the Ohara and Ichihara districts, this shopping area has provided major supplies, and is still considered "downtown" by inhabitants of the northeast areas.

Originally, the present Aoisho restaurant was the pickle-making and *kura* storehouse, and its door stands behind the register of the pickle shop. The restaurant may be entered from the shop or the entrance facing Kawaramachi-dori, where a simple white *noren* curtain hangs over the wooden sliding door. The large wooden sign above the door is written with the characters for Aoisho, the restaurant having taken its name from the nearby Aoi Bridge.

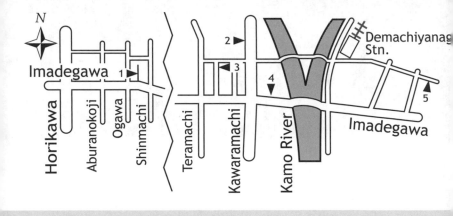

B1 Jujumaru
B2 Aoisho

B3 Demachi Rororo
B4 Bon Bon Café

B5 Falafel Garden

Thick white plaster walls have been redone and the original old beams left in place. The table-and-chair seating can hold about 40 people comfortably. The massive wooden storehouse door forms part of the inside wall. Indirect lighting and its distinct minimalist lines impart a casual and attractive atmosphere.

The unique menu offers many dishes using pickles in an innovative manner. The house specialty is *sukemono*-sushi, in which colorful slices of pickles are set on sushi rice. A small plate of tempura and red miso soup complete the meal at ¥1,200. There are other selections on the à la carte menu starting from about ¥600.

➡ West side of Kawaramachi-dori, 1 block north of Imadegawa-dori. 🕐 11:30am–3pm/5pm–10pm. 📞 075-213-3559. @ www.tanabeso.jp/aoisho. 🏠 上京区河原町今出川上ル

BON BON CAFÉ ボンボンカフェ

Café B4

This former bank is now a restaurant/café/bar featuring a high ceiling and white walls that make the interior bright and airy. The original iron grid on the outside windows is one indication of the building's former status, as is the bank vault inside, now converted to a storage area.

There is plenty of table-and-chair seating as well as a loft that is well lit and set with comfortable old chairs. A little cool in winter, a new room facing the Kamo River provides a great view of the water. (Blankets are provided for those who get chilly in the cooler months.)

The lunch menu features about four items available until 5:00 pm, after which there is an à la carte or set dinner menu. A good selection of wine and desserts rounds off the meal.

Customers should order at the counter, pay, and then find a seat. The food is served, but water and glasses are self-service.

➡️ North side of Imadegawa-dori, just east of Kawaramachi-dori. 🕐 Noon–11pm. 📞 075-213-8686. @ www.madoi-co.com/food/bon-boncafe. 🚗 中京区河原町今出川東入ル

DEMACHI RORORO 出町ろろろ

Japanese B3

This recently renovated 100-year-old house is a good example of a typical wooden neighborhood residence. The suspended ceiling has

been removed, the floor raised, and the tatami replaced with wooden flooring. A table for 4 sits against the frosted glass windows on the street side, and the counter accommodates 10. Simple rough plaster walls are a pleasant counterpoint to the dark beams and ceiling in this neat and comfortable eatery.

Only 20 lunch and dinner meals are prepared each day, after which the owners stop serving, so call ahead or arrive early if you want the daily special. The young couple running the restaurant uses produce delivered fresh from their friends' vegetable patch in Ohara, a northern suburb of Kyoto. Lunch is eight tasty tidbits served on tasteful wooden trays and comes with as many servings of rice as you like. After the meal, a wet hand towel is served on a leaf—the kind of simple touch that makes the meal all the more charming.

➡️ 1 street east of Teramachi-dori, just north of Imadegawa-dori (on east side before covered shopping street). 🕐 Noon–2pm/6pm–10pm. Closed Tuesday and 1st and 3rd Monday of month. 📞 075-213-2772. 🆁🆂🆅🅿 Recommended. 🏠 上京区今出川通り寺町東入ル一真町67-1

FALAFEL GARDEN ファラフェル ガーデン

Middle Eastern   B5

The front of this two-story shop has green-framed glass doors and a large colorful menu outside. The owner restored this 80-year-old house by replacing the tatami with large flagstones and installing a clay-walled counter in front of the kitchen. The back garden is filled with greenery, and the small room beyond the garden seats 4. Table-and-chair seating is available on both floors.

Glass windows and the removal of part of the first-floor suspended ceiling allow southern light to flow in, giving the restaurant an airy, bright feel.

Chickpeas in a pita wrap is a favorite dish, but there are many others available in large and medium size. The menu starts at ¥800, and all dishes are similarly priced.

➡ South side of street running east diagonally from Demachiyanagi Station toward Higashioji-dori. 🕐 11am–9:30pm. Closed Wednesday. 📞 075-712-1856. @ www. falafelgarden.com. 🚗 左京区田中下柳町3−16

JUJUMARU 樹樹丸

Café   B1

This 80-year-old house is a *minka*, or common person's dwelling, but the garden space, featuring an original stone lantern, is surprisingly generous for an ordinary home, showing the impor-tance the owners placed on their environment.

Jujumaru is filled with tiny bonsai, a pastime and now business venture of the young family who runs the restaurant. The new front garden exhibits plants that are for sale. Besides the garden, another charming feature of this restaurant is the door-within-a-door (*o-do* and *kuguri-do*) immediately inside the entrance.

The name was selected because it sounded good to the owners. Usually, *maru* designates a ship, but not in this case. The name can be interpreted loosely as something round and standing upright, like some of the plants on display.

The owner removed the tatami and replaced it with a plain wooden floor, so one must remove shoes to enter and sit on the floor seating.

Presently, there is a bicycle shop on the northwest corner of Imadegawa-dori, making Jujumaru easier to find in this city of many nameless streets.

The menu is casual and simple: one *teishoku*-style meal includes the main dish of the week, plus rice, soup, and pickles. A BLT sandwich is the other choice, and both selections come with tea, coffee, or juice and are priced under ¥1,000.

➡ West side of street just north of Imadegawa-dori, 1 block east of Ogawa-dori. 🕐 11am–7pm. 📞 075-432-8607. @ www.jujumaru.com. 🚗 上京区今出川通り小川東入ル西側

AME DU GARÇON アームドゥギャルソン

French   C30

Curving *inuyarai* bamboo fencing fronts the solid-looking dark wooden façade of Ame du Garçon, with the restaurant's name on a white *noren* curtain, above which is a distinctive Meiji-style lantern. This elegantly restored machiya is about 85 years old and is the

former residence of a thread merchant. All the old beams and posts have been buffed to highlight their original rich, dark hues.

The narrow stone-laid entrance has a tiled hearth (*kama*) where the former kitchen was located, the soft lighting coming from the overhead skylights. Like some Kyoto houses built around World Wars I and II, Ame du Garçon has a bomb shelter, which it has converted into an attractive wine cellar.

Ten people can sit at a sunken counter and watch the chefs skill-

MAP C • North Central Area

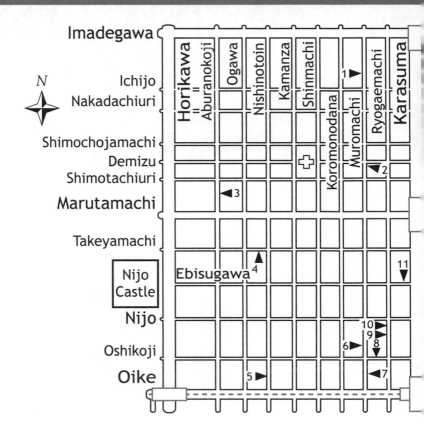

C1 Kogantei
C2 Maruko
C3 Nunoya
C4 Shiori Shiori Café
C5 Uruu
C6 Zenkashoin
C7 Ringetsu

C8 Ushinosuke
C9 Tamaki
C10 Juga
C11 Steak House Kazu
C12 Todo
C13 Kushikura
C14 Okuman Shoya

C15 Tsukitokage
C16 Nonkiya Mune
C17 Café Bibliotic
    Hello!
C18 Regalo
C19 Sarasa Oshikoji
C20 Hanamomo

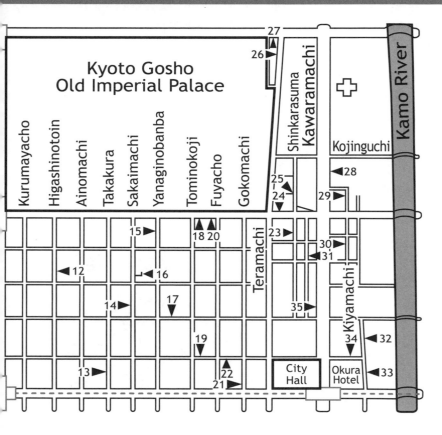

C21 El Fogon
C22 Pasta Collection
　　　House Dogetsu
C23 Café Chobitto
C24 Madam Koran
C25 Korin
C26 Epice

C27 Casa Bianca
C28 Le Pont
C29 Ital Gabon
C30 Ame du Garçon
C31 Miko
C32 Ganko
C33 Merry Island

C34 Ichi no Hunairi
C35 Very Berry Café

fully prepare the day's French cuisine. Light comes from the original frosted glass windows, and an inner garden has been completely relandscaped. Although they lack the garden view, the upstairs tatami rooms have their own charm.

➡️ West side of street 2 blocks north of Ebisugawa-dori, 1 block east of Kawaramachi-dori. 🕐 11:30am–2pm (LO)/5pm–9pm (LO). 📞 075-213-3016. 🚖 中京区中町通り夷川上ル

CAFÉ BIBLIOTIC HELLO!
カフェ ビブリオティック ハロー！

Café   **C17**

During most months, Café Bibliotic Hello! is easily recognizable by the stand of towering banana trees outside and the large glass panes that form the front wall.

The café is a 70-year-old clothing shop that now has an attached gallery. Renovations eight years ago removed the front part of the second floor, allowing sunlight to flood the restaurant. The change transformed the dark image of this traditional townhouse into a comfortable place to sit and read. The reduced second floor has two table-and-chair sets that provide customers with a delightfully personal space.

Whitewashed brick walls are an unusual find in old Japanese houses, but more than 100 years ago, when Sanjo-dori was Kyoto's Main Street, this district was a fashionable shopping area, and the brick and stone buildings provided a modern touch.

The café takes its name from the hundreds of books lining the west wall. Many are about architecture, with some in English. A cat-walk on the second floor gives access to the higher-up volumes.

The daily lunch is ¥1,000, with ¥200 extra for coffee or tea. The menu (with a wooden cover) is in English.

➡ North side of Nijo-dori, just east of Yanaginobanba-dori. 🕐 11:30am–11:30pm.
📞 075-231-8625. @ www.cafe-hello.jp. 🚗 中京区二条柳馬場東入ル晴明町

CAFÉ CHOBITTO カフェチョビット

Café	C23

Chobitto is next to towering trees that abut the Shimogoryo Shrine. Both two-story build-ings have been renovated inside while keeping their former second-floor façades. The restaurant entrance is at the back of the building via a stone pathway lined with colorful miniature bicycles that decorate the prem-ises. The Chobitto owner has constructed a stylized version of the traditional slim lattice-fronted windows, with long planks vertically placed to allow light in.

Fifties-style tables and chairs seat about 20 people. The back building is now a gallery, and a garden sits between the buildings, which features a raised platform offering extra outside seating for exhi-bitions or performances. The neighborhood has a restful, quiet feel to it, a surprise in this location, so close to downtown. Dog owners with their pets are welcome.

The daily menu is written outside on a blackboard in Japanese, but there is a menu in English inside. Lunch is around ¥1,000 (plus ¥100 for extra rice). Lunch the day I dined was a kind of Thai curry with vegetables and cheese and a small salad with sesame dressing. The other offering was a bowl of Korean *kimchi*-topped rice.

➡️ West side of Shinkarasuma-dori (1 street east of Teramachi-dori), just south of Marutamachi-dori. 🕐 Wednesday and Thursday: noon–midnight. Lunch: until 4pm. À la carte menu from 6pm. Closed Wednesday. 📞 075-213-5750. 🚗 中京区新烏丸通り丸太町下ル信富町342-2

CASA BIANCA カーサビアンカ

Italian   C27

This 100-year-old beautifully renovated former *kura* storehouse is set back from the street a house length and is identifiable by a large Italian flag visible from Imadegawa-dori. This storehouse was part of an old residence that

has since been demolished, providing parking space for the restaurant. The former wooden floor has been replaced with black tile, but otherwise, the honey-colored beams and white plaster walls remain, giving this eatery its pleasantly warm atmosphere. Although large by many storehouse standards, seating is limited, so reservations are advised.

In the airy traditional wooden structures where people lived, closets held only the futon bedding that was folded and put away each morning, freeing the tatami room for daytime activities. *Kura*, on the other hand, had thick clay walls that protected their contents, including summer mats and bamboo screens as well as textiles, seasonal clothing, art, and other treasured items.

Lunch, which includes a large salad, a choice of three pastas, and two desserts served with espresso, starts at ¥1,900.

➡ South side of Imadegawa-dori, just west of Teramachi-dori. 🕐 Noon–2pm (LO)/5pm–9:30pm (LO). Closed Monday (open if Monday is a national holiday). 📞 075-241-3023. 🔲 Recommended. @ www.casa-bianca.net. 🏠 上京区今出川通り寺町西入南側

EL FOGON エル・フォゴン

Spanish   C21

"The Fire" is the name of this Spanish-food restaurant. El Fogon is easily recognizable by its bright red frontage, *noren* curtain, and Spanish flag.

The original kitchen on the first floor is now fronted by a bar featuring a large selection of liquors lining the wall. The suspended ceiling has been removed to showcase the dark beams against the light-colored walls. A small patio with a hanging cherry tree and a few flowering plants is all that remains of the original garden.

The second floor can seat about 20 people. The beams have been exposed, and the middle section of the north wall reveals bamboo latticework and earthen clay (materials that form most traditional walls in Japan). A tiny inset of stained glass has been added for decoration. Glass doors have replaced the storage closet's paper sliding doors, and the space has been converted into a wine storage. A chart of all the regional wines in Spain on the wall nearby instructs patrons about the available selections.

Dining here is generally à la carte, and the prices are very reasonable.

→ Northwest corner of Gokomachi-dori and Oike-dori intersection. 🕐 Lunch: 11:30am–2pm. 1st-floor bar: 3pm–1am. 2nd-floor restaurant: 5pm–1am. 📞 075-221-5527. @ www.elfogon.jp. 🚕 中京区御幸町御池上がル

EPICE エビス

French   C26

Epice's atmosphere is as serene as the Kyoto Imperial Park and Palace that are directly west of the restaurant. Just over a decade ago the son of a wood carver tastefully converted this 100-year-old house into a French restaurant.

Epice, French for "spice," is pronounced "e-bi-su." The image of Ebisu, one of Japan's seven lucky gods, is carved on the sign above the traditional lattice frontage.

The tatami has been replaced with a wooden floor, so customers may wear shoes. The counter seats about 6 and the two back tables 4 each. The restaurateur's father carved the woodwork above the counter, and the panels that would ordinarily serve as transoms between rooms are now skillfully positioned to provide indirect lighting. Drawers cleverly concealed within the counter contain cutlery for a three- or four-course meal.

The inner garden with its stone lantern and year-round greenery provides a soft, inviting ambience to the dining experience, as do the interior earthen clay walls.

Lunch is between ¥2,200 and ¥3,000, and ¥300 extra for dessert.

➡ West side of Teramachi-dori, just south of Imadegawa-dori. 🕐 11:30am–2:30pm/5:30pm–9pm. Closed Wednesday. 📞 075-222-2220. @ www.kyoto-epice.jp. 🚗 上京区寺町今出川下ル

GANKO がんこ

Japanese   C32

Ganko is a well-known chain restaurant, but the Takasegawa branch is an exquisite departure, serving not only sushi but also traditional Japanese cuisine. A former villa, it was owned by statesman and two-time prime minister of Japan

Yamagawa Aritomo (1838–1922). The original estate belonged to the Suminokura family, whose patriarch, Suminokura Ryoi (1554–1614), built a canal system to move lumber products to potters in the Higashiyama Gojo area and onto Osaka markets. The Takase River, now channeled into a canal, is opposite the restaurant and part of this legacy.

Water from the Misogi River runs alongside the building, and flow from the Kamo River is diverted into streams that run through an extensive garden around the restaurant. Customers may don slippers at the garden entrance and stroll along pathways and up a rise to the separate teahouse. Attractively lit in the evenings, the garden provides a beautiful view during dining hours. Many hands helped form this green space, the most prominent being Ogawa Jihei, the landscape artist who designed the Heian Jingu garden.

The restaurant has table-and-chair seating in its front Western-style *fin de siècle* dining room. Other rooms are tatami with sunken seating and low tables. Some rooms face the exquisite main garden, others the inner garden. More than a century old, handmade glass doors with a *moiré*-like glass surface are still in use, while transom and *fusuma* sliding doors date back hundreds of years to the original estate.

Photographs of an extensive selection of reasonably priced à la carte menu items make choosing a meal easy. Set courses begin at around ¥3,000 for lunch and ¥6,000 for dinner.

➡ East side of Kiyamachi-dori, just south of Nijo-dori. ⏱ 11:30am–9pm. 📞 075-223-3456. ⟨rsvp⟩ Recommended. @ www.gankofood.co.jp. 🏠 中京区木屋町通り二条下ル東側

HANAMOMO 花もも

Noodles   C20

This tiny *soba* restaurant seats only eight down-stairs around a single table and the same number upstairs on unbordered tatami mats—a plain style of tatami often used in tearooms to indicate rusticity.

The dark, two-story building has an indigo blue and white *noren* curtain hanging in its entrance and a few potted wildflowers on the pavement outside, with a bench for those waiting to be served. Shoes are allowed on the first floor but must be removed before you climb the stairs. The second-floor tatami room has a low wooden counter for 6 and a table for 4, with all seats facing the Imperial Palace Park directly across the street.

The roughly plastered clay walls and simple pottery dishes meld with the pale *soba*, prepared fresh every day in a second-floor room. A small computer monitor downstairs shows slides of the entire process—from weighing the buckwheat flour to mixing it with water and kneading it to rolling out the dough and cutting it into thin slices—undertaken several times a day, depending on demand.

Dishes are priced from ¥900, with seasonal specials at ¥1,200.

➡ South side of Marutamachi-dori, between Tominokoji-dori and Fuyacho-dori (south side of Imperial Palace). 🕐 11am–2:30pm/5:30pm–8pm. Closed Sunday night and Monday. 📞 075-212-7787. @ www.adc-net.jp/hanamomo. 🚗 中京区丸太町麸屋町西入ル

ICHI NO HUNAIRI 一之船入

Chinese   C34

The name of the restaurant loosely means "boat berth number one." The Takase River that runs along Kiyamachi-dori was formerly used to transport goods such as charcoal and rice, as evidenced by the rice casks displayed in the shallow-

bottomed dory now docked near Nijo-dori. Behind the restaurant is a deeper section of the river used for docking.

This former *chaya* (teahouse) is about 80 years old. From the dark lattice front to the interior rooms that face the canal on the north, it has been lovingly maintained. The long, narrow structure itself was designed to allow views from most rooms. Although there is some sunken seating downstairs, all rooms upstairs are tatami and shoes are not allowed inside.

Stone flooring in the entrance and unusual red clay walls make a fine introduction to the tasteful traditional interior. The well-known Kyoto woodblock artist Clifton Karhu was fond of this eatery, and the admiration is mutual: the restaurant owner bought many of Karhu's works and has displayed some behind the lattice fronting. The second-floor rooms are intimately small with coffered ceilings, small alcoves, and attractive art, including a series of prints—now on *fusuma* paper sliding doors—that Karhu did many years ago for *Playboy* magazine.

Lunch at ¥1,500 offers a choice of five main dishes, a salad, and dessert. It does not require reservations, but the ¥3,500 lunch does, as does dinner.

➡ North side of Oshikoji-dori, just east of Kawaramachi-dori (north side of Okura Hotel). 🕐 11:30am–2pm (LO 1:30pm)/5:30pm–10pm (LO 9pm). Closed Sunday. 📞 075-256-1271. @ www.ichinohunairi.com. 🚗 中京区河原町二条下ル

ITAL GABON アイタルガボン

Italian   C29

The green tea-colored exterior walls on this two-story 80-year-old house make it distinct from all the other tradi-tionally lattice-fronted properties on this quiet side street. The neigh-borhood image of Jizo (protector of children) is at the north end of the building.

The owner, a fan of the island of Jamaica, says *gabon* means "natural" in Patois, but the little 18-seater café nevertheless serves Italian-like fare. There is a curiously named selection of felt jewelry and earrings called Debris and several bookshelves with reading material (in Japanese) for customers. The young couple live upstairs and prepare all the meals daily.

A pasta lunch is ¥900, and a gorgonzola and avocado panini sandwich is ¥800. Both come with a very fresh salad and a beverage. There is an Italian espresso machine on the counter, but Japanese beans are used.

➡ Just north of Marutamachi-dori, 1 block east of Kawaramachi-dori. ⏱ 11:30am–10pm. 📞 075-255-9053. @ italgabon.blog133.fc2.com. 🚌 上京区中町通り丸太町上ル西側

JUGA 十駕

Japanese   C10

Formerly a medicine shop, this two-story 70-year-old building was transformed by a student carpenter as his graduation thesis. The new asymmetrical doorframe, the inventive use of light, and the compactness of design reflect his sensibilites. The original *tokonoma* alcove remains, as does the borderless-tatami flooring, but it now has tables and chairs set on it. The front entrance opens to a counter that seats about 6, while the back room accommodates 16. The garden was reworked, and the old corridor leads to the restroom, still in its original place.

The name—from *juga*, a beast of burden that carries a load of boxes slowly and surely toward its destination—embodies the owner's goals. The interior is traditional as are the beautifully crafted utensils and dishes, but all are presented with a modern flair.

The cuisine is reasonably priced, with the lunch starting at ¥1,800.

West side of Ryogaemachi-dori, just south of Nijo-dori. 11:30am–4pm/5pm–10pm. Closed Monday and holidays. 075-213-2234. 中京区両替町通り二条下ル金町４７８

KOGANTEI こがん亭

Japanese   C1

Kogantei, which takes its name from a well-known local comedian, Ashiya Kogan, is easily identifiable by the *noren* curtain with a drawing of a pig, a round window, and a wooden sliding-door entrance.

Three tables and an attractive wooden counter seat about 22 people on the first floor, where there is a decorative watercolor by Ashiya Kogan.

The second floor has been converted to a large room with floor seating for 20 people who come to hear Rakugo, a popular form of humorous storytelling.

A daily menu of simple, healthy everyday Japanese food is served, most of which is accompanied by rice, pickles, and soup, all for under ¥900. Coffee is an extra ¥100.

➡ West side of Muromachi-dori, just south of Imadegawa-dori. 🕐 11:30am–4pm/5:30pm–11:30pm (LO 10:30pm). Closed Wednesday. 📞 075-432-2422. @ www.kogankurabu.com/kogantei. 🏠 上京区今出川室町下ル西側

KORIN 厚凛

Japanese   C25

Set on a quiet side street, Korin is a good example of a private residence in the neighborhood near the Imperial Palace. The house is only 70 years old but employs all the typical features of older homes: a surrounding high wall to guarantee

privacy, a large entrance, enclosed corridors on both floors, and a rather large garden, considering its inner-city location.

A simple white *noren* curtain marks the entrance into the front garden, which features a stone-inlaid path that leads from an outer wall of darkened wooden planks topped with a tile border. The rooms feature earthen clay walls, a double *tokonoma* alcove, and several lovely old chests. One upper inner window has elaborate latticework, and the transom is a handsomely carved single piece of wood. An unusual pine-needle motif decorates the lower half of the *fusuma* sliding doors, and the door pulls feature a centipede design, a family clan symbol.

The original Western-style front room has been converted into a sunken-seating counter area enclosed by glass, with a view of the outer garden.

The gardens contain large rocks arranged in pathways and in artful compositions around the grounds, reflecting the owners' wealth

and taste. Seventy years of careful grooming is evident in the beautifully matured moss-covered garden where azalea, boxwood, and
camellia bushes nestle among well-trimmed pines. A thick white-
walled *kura* storehouse sits on the southeast corner of the compound.

The seasonal Japanese menu begins at ¥1,800 for lunch and
includes appetizers of raw fish, a main dish, salad, red miso soup, and
rice with vegetables and pickles. Coffee or juice is included in the price
of lunch, but tea is ¥200 extra.

➡️ Northwest of Kawaramachi-dori and Marutamachi-dori intersection (walk north
from Teramachi-dori, turn right at 2nd corner by Niijima House; restaurant is on north
side of next corner). 🕐 11:30am–2pm (LO 1:30pm)/5:30pm–11pm (LO 10:30pm).
Closed Monday and 4th Tuesday of month. 📞 075-212-3531. 🆁🆂🆅🅿 Recommended.
🏠 上京区新烏丸太町上ル信富町２９８

KUSHIKURA くしくら

Japanese   C13

This attractive restaurant
is easy to identify by its
wooden-lattice façade
and hand-painted sign
showing the Kyoto-style
vegetables that are served
within. The 140-year-
old merchant's house has
been converted into a
spacious and popular eat-

ery featuring charcoal-roasted skewered chicken bits and grilled vegetables. The tatami flooring has sunken seating in rooms separated with
sliding *fusuma* doors. The *tori-niwa* passage that originally functioned
as the kitchen has been transformed into an attractive wooden counter
with sunken seating, behind which are shelves lined with the various

kinds of sake available. (In Japan, famous artists or calligraphers often design sake labels, adding a visual factor to the drinking experience.)

A front and a larger inner garden expand the sense of space and, when lit up at night, bathe the interior rooms in soft light.

The back storehouse has table-and-chair seating and can be rented for private parties. Reasonably priced lunch samples are displayed outside the building.

➡ West side of Takakura-dori, just north of Oike-dori. 🕐 11:30am–1:30pm /5pm–11pm (LO 10pm for food, 10:30pm for drinks). 📞 075-213-2211. @ www. fukunaga-tf.com. 🚕 中京区高倉通御池上ル西側

LE PONT ル．ポン

Canadian/Japanese   C28

Not named after the nearby Kojin Bridge as may be suspected, "The Bridge" represents the spanning of two cultures—Canada and Japan. The Japanese couple who runs Le Pont returned to Kyoto after 20 years operating in Toronto and opened this restaurant, which specializes in "Western-style" food. Most dishes reflect a Canadian taste for French and Italian ingredients, but Kyoto vegetables (*kyo-yasai*) are also prominently featured in the daily menu.

The exterior of this 120-year-old home is glass and the awning orange, as is the sign with the restaurant's name. Renovations included removing the suspended ceilings, exposing the interior beams, and installing wooden floors and a third-floor loft area used for storage.

The high ceilings on both first and second floors, dark wooden table-tops, white dishes, and bright orange accents give this space a fresh and appealing atmosphere.

Table-and-chair seating can accommodate about 25 people, and prices are very reasonable. The ¥1,500 lunch includes appetizers, a green onion soup, choice of main dish from among four selections, dessert, and coffee or tea—a very satisfying repast. There is also a very nice selection of wines. Although the menu is in Japanese, both owners speak English and will accommodate your culinary wishes as much as possible.

➡ East side of Kawaramachi-dori, just south of Kojinguchi-dori. 🕐 11:30am–2pm/5:30pm–11pm. Closed Wednesday. 📞 075-255-7207. 🏠 上京区河原町通荒神口下ル東側

MADAM KORAN マダム紅蘭

Chinese   C24

This old, two-story home is one of Kyoto's original machiya restaurants and has a distinctive black-tiled frontage. The interior retains the small rooms and features of an ordinary Japanese house, although the kitchen specializes in Chinese cuisine and the interior is pleasingly decorated with Chinese artifacts and calligraphy.

The house features a circular stairway that was highly unusual in its day. The wood used in the first-floor suspended ceiling is cypress from Kurobe on the Japan Sea side, while red cypress from Akita Prefecture forms the second-floor ceiling. Sliding *fusuma* doors patterned

with delicate interlocking gold-painted medallions have door pulls *(hikite)* shaped like plum blossoms. Both floors have tatami seating at traditional low tables.

Across the street is a well-known *soba* (buckwheat) confectionery and noodle manufacturer that owns the building; vestiges of its history—the old scales and vault—now decorate the premises.

In addition to the *ramen* dishes, a seven-course mini-*kaiseki* is served for ¥2,800 but must be ordered ahead. Delicious noodle dishes or the daily lunch, priced from ¥1,500, are served Japanese-style on low tables in tatami rooms, atypical of Chinese restaurants.

➡️ North side of Marutamachi-dori, just east of Teramachi-dori. 🕐 11:30am–2:30pm (LO 2pm)/5pm–9:30pm (LO 9pm). Closed Monday. 📞 075-212-8090. @ www.a-dos.ne.jp/gourmet/madamkouran. 🚗 中京区寺町丸太町東入ル

MARUKO まるこう

Japanese   C2

The distinctive white façade of this 100-year-old *chu-nikai* (one-and-a-half-story house) is easy to spot in its residential neighborhood.

The interior of the home has a raised tatami floor, so shoes must be taken off to enter, but the sunken seating at the red lacquer counter assures customers of comfort. Otherwise, the front room and upstairs rooms are all tatami, with a sloping front room that is typical of *chu-nikai* structures. Beautifully preserved beams and *shoji* paper windows cast a lustrous light on the second-floor rooms.

On the first floor, the white plaster walls present a striking contrast to the dark-stained ceiling. A small back garden with a stone lantern and water basin brings in a little light, but otherwise, the softly lit interior imbues the space with an intimate feeling.

Because of three nearby hotels, the restaurateur has prepared an English menu; the seasonal delicacies are written in Japanese on papers hanging from the walls, so ask for help if you wish to indulge in some of these dishes. The owner is from the Japan Sea–facing prefecture of Ishikawa, so seafood is a specialty.

Lunch courses begin at a very reasonable ¥800 and come with tempura, a choice of vegetable, soup, and rice.

➡ Southeast corner of Demizu-dori and Muromachi-dori intersection, south of YWCA. 🕐 11:30am–2pm/5pm–11pm. Closed Sunday. 📞 075-406-0760. 🚗 上京区室町通り出水下ル

MERRY ISLAND メリー・アイランド

Café   C33

One can see all the way through this casual eatery to its back garden with outside seating. In warm months, the front doors open to Kiyamachi-dori, making the café an excellent place for people watching. The suspended ceiling has been removed  and the raised tatami flooring replaced with rough wooden-plank dark-stained flooring, increasing the height and space of the interior and giving the café a warm, organic feel. In warm months the doors are removed and seating is extended to the willow-lined street. One of the major charms of machiya restaurants is their gardens, an open space not sacrificed for more seating but preserved to honor the integrity of design and a bygone lifestyle.

Merry Island's food is casual with many pasta offerings, seafood dishes, salads, and a good variety of desserts for mid-afternoon tea time. The café specializes in decorative cappuccino foam art, a skill beautifully rendered by the steady hand of one of the female staff. A chalkboard menu lists seasonal offerings, and food is reasonably priced, with dishes starting at about ¥1,000.

➜ East side of Kiyamachi-dori, just north of Oike-dori. 🕐 11:30am–3pm/6pm–11pm. Closed Monday. 📞 075-213-0214. 🚗 中京区木屋町通御池上ル

MIKO みこう

Japanese   C31

This former lumber store has been transformed into a lovely *kaiseki* restaurant. For centuries, lumber and charcoal were transported west to east along Marutamachi–dori ("log street") to Kiyama-chi ("wood district"), supplying the enter-tainment districts with

charcoal for heating and cooking and the Gojo district with cords of wood for the pottery kilns there. One lumber shop still exists on this little street, giving credence to the former existence of others.

A simple white *noren* curtain hangs outside the dark wooden-lattice front of this two-story building, indicating it is open for dining. The front half of the restaurant with table-and-chair seating was originally where lumber was stored, so this area is quite large. The rooms farther back offer tatami seating.

Interior wooden surfaces are polished to a dark sheen, as are the traditional chests and sliding closet doors in the entrance. The black-lacquered tables in the front room have a lustrous red lacquer stripe running down their centers, providing a vivid parallel to the red-lac-quered trays on which the traditional cuisine is served.

Kaiseki is the most elegant and traditional form of Japanese cuisine, and each beautifully presented and delicate-tasting ingredient at Miko corresponds to the current season. The two-tiered lunch box is served with a bowl of rice, clear soup, and for dessert, a scoop of creamy green-tea ice cream. Because *kaiseki* is so labor intensive, the price is often expensive, so sampling this cuisine for lunch (which runs about ¥2,500) is a wise choice for beginners.

➡ 2 blocks south of Marutamachi-dori (or 1 block north of Ebisugawa-dori), just west of Kawaramachi-dori on east side of street. 🕐 11:30am–2:30pm/5:30pm–9:30pm. Closed Monday (unless Monday is a national holiday) and 3rd Tuesday of month. 📞 075-221-4826. 🏠 中京区河原町通川夷川西入一筋上ル

NONKIYA MUNE 呑喜屋むね

Japanese   C16

This commoner's house is 80 years old with an entrance easily identi-fied by its earthen-colored clay walls with a white-pebble ground border and wooden sliding door. The long

narrow interior mostly consists of a long counter that can seat 12 and two small table-and-chair sets. Visible at the back is a garden that has been relandscaped with a maple tree and a solitary rock resting on soft mounds of star moss—a very refreshing backdrop that the owners decided to keep rather than remove to increase seating.

The owners busily prepare the day's set lunch, a very reasonable selection of Japanese dishes served on a tray. Bottles of *shochu*, a liquor made from sweet potato and a specialty of the island of Kyushu, line the wall behind the bar.

➡️ Down narrow alleyway, east off Sakaimachi-dori, just north of Ebisugawa-dori. 🕐 Noon–2pm/5:30pm–10pm. Closed Sunday. 📞 075-241-3210. 🚗 中京区堺町通夷川上ル絹屋町127-5

NUNOYA 布屋

Café   C3

Slightly out of the downtown area, this 120-year-old townhouse was lovingly renovated into a restaurant and bed and breakfast. The dark lattice front has the traditional *mushiko-mado* clay-lattice window and an image of Shoki-san,

the demon queller, mounted on the wall. The building was originally a shop that sold mosquito netting, a gauzy, tent-like covering with which Japanese would enclose their futons during the hot and humid summer nights. While renovating, the owner found a steel plate with the name *nuno* ("cloth") stamped on it—hence, the restaurant's name.

A simple menu of curry rice, soup and a sandwich, or a cake and beverage set is mounted outside on a stand beside the *noren* curtain. Shoes may be worn at the table-and-chair seating in the cool, dark interior. One raised room is provided for guests who feel more comfortable sitting on tatami. In the main room, three handsome wooden tables are set apart enough to make the room feel spacious, and traditional furniture, especially the large *mizuya*, enhances the atmosphere of this machiya. Even the food is served on the kind of blue and white dishes favored in old Kyoto homes.

In the back garden, an original stone lantern and large *tsukubai* stone basin are nestled in greenery.

Visitors can stay overnight in one of two upstairs rooms for the reasonable rate of ¥8,800.

➡ East side of Aburanokoji-dori, just north of Marutamachi-dori, opposite and south of Ando Doll Shop. 🕐 Noon–6pm. Closed Monday and 3rd Tuesday of month. 📞 075-211-8109. @ www.nunoya.net. 🚗 上京区油小路丸太町上ル

OKUMAN SHOYA 奥満笑屋

Japanese
C14

Horino Kinenkan is the carefully preserved 1820 home of the man who established the Kinshi Masumune sake brewery. About 20 other breweries once existed in the vicinity, drawing water from the area's abundant natural springs. Now, instead of sake (which is still

produced in Fushimi), three types of beer are brewed in the traditional storehouse just west of the parking lot. To the left of the storehouse/brewery is Okuman Shoya, a small but quite good restaurant featuring Japanese food. The name means "a shop full of laughter," and after trying the types of sake and beer available, customers are sure to leave smiling. With only 15 or so seats, Okuman Shoya is but a small part of the entire compound. Pay an additional ¥300 to get a tour of the house that includes sake and beer-tasting.

All dishes on the Okuman Shoya menu are of a quality found in fine sushi bars and are presented just as beautifully. There are reasonably priced lunches from ¥1,000. Some of the courses are tempura, raw fish, and sushi, with soup, rice and pickles. Selections from the à la carte menu are served at night.

➡ West side of Sakaimachi-dori, just north of Nijo-dori (through parking lot for Horino Kinenkan). 🕐 11:30am–3pm/5pm–11pm. Closed Monday. 📞 075-223-2073. 🏠 京区境界町通り二条上がル西側

PASTA COLLECTION HOUSE DOGETSU

パスタコレクションハウス 道月

Italian	C22

Dogetsu provides a satisfying repast for pasta lovers. The young Italian chef uses sauces lightly and with flair. The Japanese owner bought and remodeled the 100-year-old two-story house, leaving many original features in place. There are three rooms with table-and-chair seating, but the clay walls and sliding paper *fusuma* doors with typical Kyoto-style motifs like stylized clouds, flying plovers, and willows add a genteel touch.

The outside lattice front has been glass lined, allowing light to pour in while keeping the temperature inside comfortable. The sliding lattice door entrance opens to a Western-style front room with original tile flooring. In the early part of the 20th century, it became fashionable to welcome guests into a Western-style room with upright chairs, a novelty at the time.

One interior wall features a staggered shelf alcove, whose lowest shelf provides bench seating for the tables nearest it. Light pours in from a small *tsubo-niwa* garden between this room and the raised tatami back rooms that face a larger inner garden, or *oku-no-niwa*. The kitchen remains in its former site but has been completely modernized. The elaborate inner doors, fine clay walls, suspended wooden ceilings, and ornamental wood in the alcove show the former owner's wealth.

A back room is raised and shoes must be removed here, but the tatami has been covered with carpet, allowing for table-and-chair seating. A middle room seats 6, making a total of about 30 seats.

The first course is an appetizer (tuna or roast beef the day I went), followed by two pasta courses, one short and one long, each with a choice of sauces. One dessert and the restaurant's special blend of peach and Earl Grey tea are included in the ¥1,500 lunch course. Espresso or cappuccino is an extra ¥200, and those who wish to sample more of their luscious desserts can do so for an additional ¥600. Dinner is around ¥3,000.

➡ Southeast corner of Fuyacho-dori and Oshikoji-dori. 🕐 11:30am–2pm /5:30pm–9pm. 📞 075-253-1185. @ www.dougetsu.com. 🚗 中京区押小路麩屋町東南角橘町616

REGALO レガーロ

Italian	C18

This Italian-style restaurant was opened by a young man from the north of Japan who brings a distinctive style to his dishes. The sliding door in the traditional dark-stained wooden-lattice front is original and opens to a small room that was once the entrance but now has table-and-chair seating. The inner room also has

table-and-chair seating; a large gold-foil painted screen mounted along the wall adds a touch of elegance. Light comes from the glass-enclosed lattice front and small back garden. Lunch starts at ¥800 and dinner at ¥2,500.

➡ South side of Marutamachi-dori, 2 blocks east of Teramachi-dori (south side of Imperial Palace). 🕐 11:30am–2pm/5:30pm–9pm. Closed Wednesday. 📞 075-257-7337. 🏠 中京区丸太町富小路通り東ル

RINGETSU　凛月

Japanese　　　　　　　　　　　　　　　　　　　　C7

This two-story restaurant has a lattice covering half of its frontage. A *noren* curtain hangs over the entrance. As with the other houses on Muro-machi-dori, this 70-year-old home belonged to a clothier whose shop was in the front room. This

space now has two-table seating while the upstairs rooms have seating on the wooden floor. Light comes from a small inner garden with a stone lantern and a bit of greenery.

Lunches are simple yet fine classical fare served on fan-shaped trays. The fish is excellent. The daily lunch for ¥1,200, is very reasonable. Other selections start around ¥800. There is one lunch daily with all the sake you can drink for ¥2,000.

➡️ East side of Muromachi-dori, just north of Oike-dori. 🕐 Noon–2pm/5:30pm–11pm. Closed for lunch Sunday and Monday. 📞 075-211-2513. 🚗 中京区室町通り御池上ル

SARASA OSHIKOJI サラサ押小路

Café	C19

This Sarasa restaurant specializes in pancakes and, like the others, retains the charm of the space it occupies. The building is a *chu-nikai* (one-and-a-half-story house); the upper floor has a vertical clay-lattice window (*mushiko-mado*). The downstairs façade has been replaced with sliding glass doors to admit more light. The interior has been gutted and tatami removed. Table-and-chair seating accommodates about 30 customers when counter stools are included. The kitchen ceiling rises up to the skylight in the roof just as it used to in every traditional home.

A back garden has a few trees; their leafy limbs are a treat in an inner-city dwelling. The middle upstairs room has been removed and replaced with a solid catwalk that connects the leaf-viewing room and a room with a steeply slanted ceiling.

Lunch starts at ¥1,000 for sausage, a slice of ham, salad platter served with 3 pancakes, and coffee or tea. Coffee with two pancakes for ¥500 is available from 8:00 am to 11:30 am, after which the lunch menu starts. Desserts are pancake-based, but there also is apple pie and cheesecake from ¥600.

➡️ North side of Oshikoji-dori, just east of Tominokoji-dori. 🕐 8am–10pm (LO 9pm). Sunday: 8am–8pm (LO 7pm). Closed Wednesday. 📞 075-241-4884. @ sarasao.exblog.jp. 🏠 中京区押小路富小路東入ル橘町630

SHIORI SHIORI CAFÉ 栞栞カフェ

Japanese   C4

This two-story 120-year-old building is double the width of a usual house and was probably a merchant's home. The restaurant is recognizable by a dark lattice exterior with glass windows across the second floor, a blue *noren* curtain and sign

with the café's name, and a potted olive tree beside the menu black-boards outside.

Shiori Shiori is on Takeyamachi-dori, meaning "bamboo-shop street," one block south of Marutamachi-dori ("log street"), along which lumber was carted across town from west to east to be shipped down the Takase River. Bamboo was also brought into the city via this route. In the Edo period, however, many kinds of shops lined this street, notably those of carpenters who supplied the imperial court located in Gosho and the Nijo Castle with bamboo and metal utensils and, later, the furniture makers along Ebisugawa-dori.

The entire house has been gutted, exposing the large beams on the second floor, giving this eatery an open, spacious feel. The tatami has been replaced with wooden flooring, and downstairs there is a long metal-covered wooden counter with high stools that seat 6, two tables, and a new room for private parties. Downstairs can seat 15, and upstairs 25. A glass case displaying the dessert selections is near the entrance, and a back garden brings in a bit of light and greenery to the rustic interior. Attractive stained glass windows soften the mood and add a bit of privacy.

Brown rice is the staple with every meal. The beverage menu has the usual listing of drinks, but there also is a selection of *koji* rice malt beverages as well as soya drinks. Breakfast is ¥500 with either an egg and toast, or an egg over a bowl of steaming rice with miso soup and coffee, tea, or juice.

The daily *obanzai* (homemade dishes) is ¥680 and includes a selection of cooked vegetables with brown rice, miso soup, and pickles, all organically grown. Beverages are ¥210 extra with lunch, and homemade cakes are around ¥500.

➡️ South side of Takeyamachi-dori, just west of Nishinotoin-dori. 🕐 9:30am–6:30pm. Breakfast: 9:30am–11:30am. Lunch: 11:30am–2:30pm. 📞 075-221-6699. 🏠 中京区尾張町203-2

STEAK HOUSE KAZU　ステーキハウスカズ

Japanese　　　　　　　　　　　　　　　　　　　C11

Steak House Kazu is a two-story building with a dark-lattice frontage. Downstairs has table-and-chair seating for 16 with an attractive curved counter for 8 in the back. The front is lit from the south-facing

window looking out on a tiny front garden (*tsubo-niwa*), while a larger back garden with a stone basin, lantern, and steppingstones provides a verdant backdrop to those seated at the counter. Both gardens are new, a testimony to the Japanese preference for garden landscapes over extra seating.

One large tatami room, reserved for parties, seats about 20 on the second floor.

The lunch menu has combination dishes of fish and beefsteak or hamburger served with miso soup, rice, and pickles—a hearty lunch for ¥850. Coffee is an extra ¥150. The menu states that its more expensive grilled steak is prepared on a very-high-fired, dense beechwood charcoal, guaranteed to enhance the distinctive taste of the beef.

➡ North side of Ebisugawa-dori, several houses west of Karasuma-dori. 🕐 11:30am–2pm (LO)/5:30pm–11pm (LO 9:30pm). Closed Monday. 📞 075-708-6110. 🚗 中京区夷川通り烏丸西入ル

TAMAKI たま妓

French   C9

Tamaki's handsome lattice frontage reveals a small garden with table and chairs that is part of the café. This old merchant's home was restored by a Tokyo woman whose dream was to run a restaurant in a traditional Kyoto house.

She has kept the beautiful garden as the focus of the rooms. A Meiji-style lantern is mounted above the *noren* curtain over the entrance. The tatami flooring has been outfitted with low tables and chairs so

that diners may enjoy the French cuisine in comfort. All the courses are served on antique Japanese dishes in lacquered boxes. The old *shoji* paper doors, transoms, and clay and plaster walls soften the interior lighting.

The original shop front is now a café with table-and-chair seating and a view of a smaller garden. There are many kinds of tea on the menu, with prices starting at ¥800. The "Kyomachiya" lunch is eight courses at ¥2,700.

→ West side of Ryogaemachi-dori, just south of Nijo-dori. 🕐 11:30am–2pm/5pm–10pm (LO 9pm). Café: 2pm–4:30pm. Closed Wednesday. 📞 075-213-4177. rsvp Required. @ www.tamaki-kyoto.com. 🚗 中京区両替町通り二条下ル金吹町472番地の1

TODO 東洞

Italian	C12

A stone-like façade forms the lower half of the outer wall, an architectural feature used in some homes built about 80 years ago. A lattice wooden door is at the entrance, with clear panes on the street-facing side. An open wooden stair-

way has replaced the former steep and narrow one that most old homes still have (and that people must descend sideways). The tatami have been replaced with finely laid paneled wooden flooring. Light comes from street-facing windows and the back garden, nicely illuminating the black walls and ceiling. Exposed beams have been reinforced but remain visible. Tables and chairs on both floors means that guests can keep their shoes on while dining. There are two lunch specials: the ¥2,100 lunch includes an appetizer, soup, choice of pasta, dessert, and coffee or tea; the ¥3,500 lunch includes an entrée of fish or meat.

Small and cozy, the restaurant seats about 30 people.

➡ East side of Higashinotoin-dori, 2 blocks south of Marutamachi-dori (look for green banner). 🕐 11:30am–2pm/5:30pm–10pm. Closed Thursday. 📞 075-212-5207. @ www.mrmd.co.jp/toudou. 🏠 中京区東洞院竹屋町下ル三本五町目４９６番地３

TSUKITOKAGE ツキトカゲ

Japanese   C15

This 100-year-old home is set back one full house length from the street. The name means "lizard in the moon," as pictured on the sign in the entrance. The interior has been renovated by taking out the tatami flooring but keeping the

old earthen walls and pillars. Potted green plants give the restaurant a tropical Caribbean feel that is reflected in the names of the cocktails on the menu. A garden with a few outside chairs is where the original house once stood.

Lunch starts from ¥800. A special Japanese set course is ¥2,625.

➡ West side of Yanaginobanba-dori, just south of Marutamachi-dori and Imperial Park. 🕐 11:30am–3pm/5pm–11pm. Closed Wednesday. 📞 075-212-3550. @ www.tsukitokage-honten.com. 🏠 中京区柳馬場丸太町下ル4丁目

URUU うるう

Uruu's 100-year-old house has a handsome dark-stained lattice exterior. The tatami floor has been removed and replaced with a counter for 6 and sofa seating for 6 around a low table, giving the interior a homey lived-in setting.

The second floor has tables and chairs on carpeted flooring. The original *tokonoma* alcove has been preserved, indicating family quarters were here while the downstairs must have been used for business. Exposed beams have been beautifully reworked and restained to show off the quality of the wood grain. The back garden has a table and chairs.

Uruu-doshi means "leap year." Apparently it was an Italian custom for the local lord to close the gate to his estate every February 29 to escape the duties of his office: a respite from governing. The name was adopted to mean that customers can retreat here from their daily lives for a simple but tasty Italian meal.

➡️ West side of Nishinotoin-dori, just north of Oike-dori. 🕐 11:30am–2:30pm (LO 2pm)/5:30pm–11pm. Café: 11:30am–4pm. 📞 075-211-0724. @ www.mrmd.co.jp/uruu. 🚗 中京区西洞院御池上ル西側

USHINOSUKE 牛の助

Japanese/Korean   C8

The dark wooden-lattice-fronted townhouse has a lighter-colored wooden-lattice sliding door behind a short *noren* curtain at the entrance. The 100-year-old house belonged to a clothier, and much of the original structure remains but with new interior walls and lighting. Two small tatami rooms seat about 6 each and have views of a small garden. Another room has sunken seating for 4 and counter seating for 6.

The fare is a mix of Japanese and Korean beef dishes. An English menu is available. The ¥850 lunch special is of Japanese *sukiyaki* beef, soup, tofu, and a vegetable salad. The drinks menu has a surprisingly large amount of spirits, *makkoli* (Korean rice wine) being one of the more unusual selections.

➡️ North side of Oshikoji-dori, just west of Ryogaemachi-dori. 🕐 11:30am–2:30pm (LO 2pm)/5pm–10:30pm (LO 10pm). 📞 075-223-2539. @ www.ushinosuke.com.
🚇 中京区押小路通室町東入ル蛸薬師町292-3

VERY BERRY CAFÉ

Café   C35

The former location of a lumber dealer, Very Berry is a sturdy 100-year-old two-story building with vertical clay windows (*mushiko-mado*) across the second floor and attractive curving bamboo fencing (*inuyarai*) on the ground floor. This area once had a number of lumber yards that sold timber transported from the western areas of Kyoto across Marutamachi-dori ("log street") to be shipped down the canal from Nijo-dori that flows along Kiyamachi-dori. The logs were used to

fire the kilns of the potters living in the Gojo area and as charcoal for heating and cooking throughout the entertainment districts of Pontocho, Shinbashi, Gion, and Miyazawa-cho. The original dealer at this location specialized in exotic woods, most likely used as decorative touches in Kyoto's wooden homes.

Asked why the café has the name "Very Berry," one staff said that it is difficult for Japanese to differentiate between "v" and "b," so they decided to give their customers a pronunciation challenge.

The tatami has been removed to allow table-and-chair seating inside this smoke-free café. The large interior is separated by a stairway that leads to a "children's room" on the second floor where young mothers and their children can relax without disturbing others. A large flat-screen video keeps the kiddies occupied while the toddlers sprawl around in the tatami room next to the *mushiko-mado* window. The menu notes that cats and dogs are allowed to accompany their owners.

A back garden provides more light than greenery for the first floor. The menu carries a large variety of sweet items: homemade cakes and dishes such as French toast with ice cream and pancake sundaes. Lunches are simple pasta dishes and two kinds of sandwiches: BLT and ham and cream cheese, both priced about ¥900 including coffee or tea. Dinner is from ¥950.

➡️ West side of Kawaramachi-dori, just north of Nijo-dori. 🕐 11:30am–midnight. Lunch: 11:30am–4pm. Dinner: 5pm–11pm. 📞 075-231-5002. @ www.veryberry. jp. 🚃 中京区河原町二条上ル西側

ZENKASHOIN 然花抄院

This venerable 290-year-old house has one of the longest frontages north of Oshikoji-dori on the west side of Muromachi-dori.

The very large white *noren* curtain uses contemporary calligraphy to present the single character *zen*, meaning "nature." This stark and abstract minimalist style is echoed throughout the shop, starting with the black curved *inuyarai* fencing, a modern version of the softly curved bamboo fencing seen in older houses. Solid white plaster walls form the second-floor frontage.

This home once belonged to a clothier, and it was one of the grandest in Kyoto. Today it is the location of a traditional sweets maker that specializes in many kinds of confectioneries used in the tea ceremony. Another of its specialties is a type of *castella* cake. *Castella* was introduced into Japan during the 16th century by the Portuguese living in Kyushu. The name comes from Pan de Castela, "bread from Castile." The Japanese took this recipe to heart, and today it remains a very popular cake available in most supermarkets. Zenkashoin's *castella* (¥800) has a sweet creamy filling, unlike the Kyushu variety that resembles a light-tasting sponge cake.

Inside the cake shop is the old vault used in the original merchant's business and a *kura* storehouse that has been converted into a room that seats 6. The middle garden has a single cherry and maple tree on a flat square of green, as contemporary in design as the abstract curtain hanging at the entrance.

The gallery in back displays items designed by the owner's daughter, whose artwork decorates the walls in both structures. Inside the gallery is an old well next to a black brick fireplace with huge cauldrons that once fed not only the family but also, as was customary, all employees. The beam to the immediate right of the gallery entrance notes the date of construction 290 years ago.

Visitors are free to enter and visit the shop and gallery and see the immense infrastructure of beams and posts.

➡ West side of Muromachi-dori, just south of Nijo-dori. ⏱ 10am–7pm. Closed Monday (closed Tuesday if Monday is a national holiday). 📞 075-241-3300. @ www.zen-kashoin.com. 🚗 中京区室町通り二条下ル蛸薬師町271-1

ALTRETTANTO アルトレタント

Italian   D28

A Kyoto landmark, this
120-year-old renovated
townhouse belongs to
Kishimatsumine Sake,
whose name is still visible
along the outside wall.
Sturdy and atmospheric,
this machiya grand dame
is representative of many
of the old businesses that

used to exist in the downtown area.

A *mushiko-mado* window with rounded wooden poles instead of
the usual clay-lattice slats has been preserved, while the lattice frontage
has been replaced with glass to brighten the front rooms. An interior
garden brings light and greenery to seating in back. The front entrance
has retained its original inset stone floor. Farther back, a raised wooden
floor provides seating for about 30 and is non-smoking. The second
floor is for smokers, with wooden flooring and larger tables for parties
and special events. A highlight of the Italian cuisine is the excellent

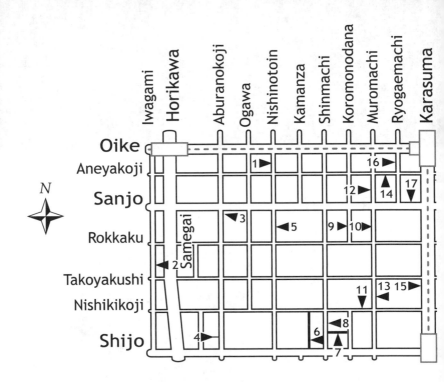

D1 Marukyu Koyamaen
D2 Ratna Café
D3 Odekakebiyori
D4 Kyotomi-an
D5 Il Pozzo
D6 Yururiya
D7 Sugari
D8 Amedio
D9 Orto

D10 What's
D11 Zezekan Pocchiri
D12 Ao
D13 Maeda Coffee
D14 Corno Rosso
D15 Flowing
D16 Kusabi
D17 Due
D18 Ask a Giraffe

D18 Kilala
D18 Papa Jon's New
    York Eatery
D18 Shinpuhkan
D18 Tawawa
D19 O-mo-ya
    Higashinotoin
D20 Second House
    Higashinotoin

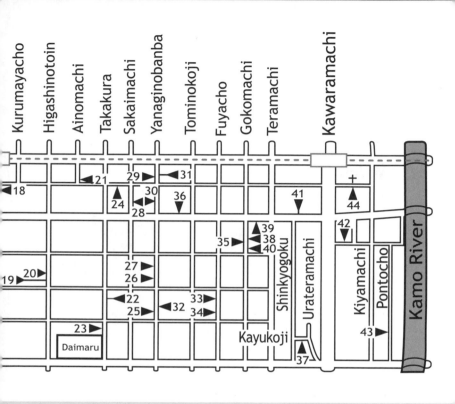

D21 Mimadeli
D22 Enya
D23 Kin no Tsubasa
D24 Kosendo
D25 Gogyo
D26 Saikontan
D27 Kichijojo
D28 Altrettanto
D29 Machiya Yu

D30 Chisoinaseya
D31 Quarirengué
D32 Ichi no Den
D33 Itadori
D34 Omo Café
D35 Okudohan
D36 Ushi no Hone
D37 Sarasa Kayukoji
D38 Kokoroya

D39 Café Chocolat
D40 Cinq Ryokan and
    Café
D41 Katsukura
D42 En
D43 Ranman
D44 Otonari

thin-crust pizza prepared in Altrettanto's authentic stone oven. Lunches begin at ¥1,200 with a choice of several pasta dishes or pizza; coffee or tea is ¥200 extra. A selection of desserts is also available.

➡️ East side of Sakaimachi-dori, just north of Sanjo-dori. 🕐 11:30am–3pm/5pm–10pm. Closed Monday. 📞 075-253-3339. @ www.altrettanto.com/. 🚗 中京区境界町通り三条上ル東側

AMEDIO アメディオ

Italian   D8

This 100-year-old *chu-nikai* (one-and-a-half-story house) has been half converted into an Italian restaurant. Its mixed heritage is reflected in a white *noren* curtain hanging alongside a small Italian flag on the first-floor tile eave. Instead of the typical frontage of vertical latticework, Amedio has blocked squares of vertical and horizontal latticework. The second floor clay-lattice windows (*mushiko-mado*) have been replaced with sliding glass ones, traversed by two lengths of darkened bamboo. The thick wooden beam in the entrance's tatami room has been incorporated into the counter, along with a thick plate of glass. On the wall behind hangs an image of Amedio, the Italian character for which this restaurant is named.

Tables and chairs in a small back room sit 8; the counter can accommodate 6, with room for another 12 upstairs, where unusually shaped overhead beams are set off by white plaster walls and street-facing windows. The dark gleaming finish of the wooden interior imparts a warm and cozy atmosphere.

This tiny restaurant fills half of the original structure, with the owners still living in the back.

The lunch menu offers three choices: *A* at ¥1,200, *B* ¥1,500, and *C* ¥2,500. *A* consists of an appetizer, a choice of five pasta dishes, and dessert. *B* and *C* choices include more dishes. Coffee, tea, or espresso is an extra ¥200 with the meal.

➡ East side of Shinmachi-dori, just north of Shijo-dori. 🕐 11am–3pm (LO 2pm)/5:30pm–11pm (LO 10pm). Closed Tuesday. 📞 075-223-3339. @ www. amedio.info. 🚖 中京区新町四条上ル東側

AO レストラン蒼

French   D12

This 140-year-old former merchant's house (*shoka*) is an example of the tasteful restoration of a business/residence. One generation removed from the kimono business, the present manager is the grandson of the founder. The beauty of this restaurant—spacious, light, and airy with a pale wooden interior and large glass-enclosed garden—lies in its rich blend of exotic interior materials, now within a casual setting.

Muromachi-dori has a 1,200-year-old history and is the old capital's only continually trodden street. Extending from Kitayama-dori all the way south to Jujo, the street is closely connected to the textile business. Some 450 shops devoted to weaving and dyeing dot the area between Oike-dori and Gojo-dori. The wealth of some of the

Muromachi merchants is reflected in large compounds called *shoka*, or merchant houses, that remain. Originally, the street-facing rooms were used for business, while special guests were invited into the inner back rooms, which included architectural features such as transoms (*ramma*) and alcoves (*tokonoma*). The family lived upstairs.

At Ao, two thick-walled storehouses (*kura*) connected by a stone walkway were once used to house merchandise but now serve as boutiques. The back outer patio area is one of the few places where Kyotoites may dine accompanied by their pets.

The formal front garden with its standing stone lantern can be viewed from the street as well as inside. A contemporary flower arrangement in the garden offsets the more traditional moss and fern greenery.

The cuisine is a fusion of Japanese and French, incorporating fresh Kyoto vegetables (*kyo-yasai*). Lunch is from ¥3,500.

➡ West side of Muromachi-dori, just north of Sanjo-dori. 🕐 11:30am–3pm (LO 2pm)/5:30pm–10pm (LO 9pm). Closed Wednesday and 1st Tuesday of month. 📞 075-221-7775. @ www.kyotoism-ao.com. 🚗 中京区室町三条上ル

ASK A GIRAFFE アスク ア ジラフ

Café	D18

This popular café is on the first floor of Shinpuh-kan, which once served as the offices of Nippon Telegraph and Tele-phone. The entrance to Ask a Giraffe is from the main courtyard or the adjoining shop. Eclectic, modern furniture pro-

vides seating for couples and foursomes. Appropriate to the building's former role, the floor space is generous and the ceiling high (thus the café's name).

Lunch is about ¥900 with ¥100 extra for soup or pasta salad. There is an enticing selection of cakes that are made on the premises, insuring a steady appreciative clientele throughout the day.

See also the entry for Shinpuhkan.

➡️ 1st floor of Shinpuhkan building, on southeast corner of Aneyakoji-dori and Karasuma-dori. 🕐 11am–11pm. 📞 075-213-6688. @ www.shinpuhkan.jp/ category/restaurant/ask_a_giraffe. 🚕 中京区烏丸通り姉小路下ル場之町

CAFÉ CHOCOLAT カフェショコラ

French/Italian   D39

Windows that let in lots of sunlight and a high ceiling give this second-floor café a bright, spacious atmosphere. The three-story old Mainichi Newspaper Building, built in 1928, has been partially renovated, so there are no handrails on the winding narrow stairs. The rough plaster walls have been painted white, and oil paintings (some for sale) line the walls. A large oval table in the center of the café seats at least 10, with plenty of table-and-chair seating along the walls. Alcoves offer a bit of privacy for small parties.

The menu is in English and Japanese, featuring many à la carte dishes, with French and Italian cuisine equally represented with the ubiquitous pasta favorites. The "cake set" (pronounced "kay-key-set-tow"), a selection of desserts and a beverage, is ¥1,050.

➡️ Southeast corner of Sanjo-dori and Gokomachi-dori (entrance on Sanjo-dori side). 🕐 11:30am–11pm (LO 11pm). 📞 075-211 2357. @ www.cafechocolat.cc. 🚗 中京区三条御幸町東入ル弁慶石町56,1928ビル2F

CHISOINASEYA 馳走いなせや

Japanese   **D30**

Chiso means "delicious," and *inase* means "a dapper man-about-town," so a loose translation of *Chisoinaseya* would be "delicious dandy dishes." A visit here guarantees a hearty meal served in attractive dishes by waitresses dressed in kimono-style uniforms. The restaurant is in a house behind a house, down a narrow pathway covered with green rectangular tiles with the names of many of Kyoto's districts (*cho*) written on them in a pale green glaze. A signboard with photos of the restaurant's interior and a list of available dishes is on the right side of the entrance. The pathway wall is covered in a thick fence of twigs and branches, a divider occasionally used in traditional Japanese gardens.

The 60-year-old building originally had a Western-style entry, now part of the kitchen and front entrance. The restaurant seats 25, with sunken seating for 8 in the *kura* storehouse in the very back of the compound and along the counter. Shoes must be removed; low wooden-backed seats are arranged on a gleaming floor.

Old wooden doors have been incorporated into the renovation, and the garden has been remade with steppingstones and stone lanterns along the southern and western sides.

All dishes are chicken based, prepared with a marvelously delicious broth. I had the white *miso-ramen* noodles dish, served in a thick, darkly glazed earthenware bowl, for ¥880. The daily lunch, steamed chicken on rice with a separate pot of broth and condiments for the customer to mix into the rice, is ¥1,200. Other lunch items were around ¥1,200, the most expensive lunch being ¥2,500.

➡ West side of Yanaginobanba-dori, just north of Sanjo-dori. 🕐 11:30am–2pm (LO)/5pm–10:30pm (LO). 📞 075-255-7250. @ homepage3.nifty.com/chisouinaseya. 🏠 中京区柳馬場道り三条上ル西側

CINQ RYOKAN AND CAFÉ サンクカフェ

Café D40

This two-story building still retains the sign from the time it was the Tanaka Inn. The earthen exterior wall has a modern lattice window to the right of the door and slender bamboo trees on the left. A chalkboard has "Lunch Menu" printed in English, but individual items are written in Japanese. The downstairs operates as a café that serves a few dishes, mainly pasta and curry rice, and cake and coffee sets are also available, the chocolate torte being a local specialty.

One tatami room remains in front, but shoes can be worn in the rest of the café, which has table-and-chair seating for about 30 people. A small back garden brings in light, and the suspended ceiling has been removed and covered in white plaster. The café has one back room, divided by sliding reed doors that allow air to circulate while offering diners a bit of privacy. Paper floor lamps soften the interior lighting, and potted plants give the café a simple and warm atmosphere.

Most dishes are about ¥1,050, and the staff will explain them to you.

The second floor has been divided into four luxurious bedrooms with private baths. Rooms start at about ¥15,000 a night.

➡️ East side of Gokomachi-dori, just south of Sanjo-dori. 🕐 Lunch: noon–2:30pm. Dinner: 6pm–9:30pm. Café: noon–11pm. 📞 075-708-7949. @ www.ctn139.com.
🚗 中京区三条御幸町下ル海老屋町

CORNO ROSSO コルノロッソ

Italian   D14

This clothier's home is 80 years old and has been completely renovated, so although its interior is new, the size and dimensions are as long and narrow as when the original family lived in this two-story dwelling. The front has new lattice

windows that retain this machiya's traditional look. Light from a rear garden of white gravel, a few large stones, and a *nanten* plant brightens up a small, windowed back room that can seat a private party of 6.

The counter seats 6, and table-and-chair seating can accommodate 12.

Weekday lunch is a choice of pasta dishes with a small salad for ¥1,200. Coffee is an extra ¥100, and dessert, ¥300. Prices and menus differ on the weekend.

➡️ South side of Aneyakoji-dori, just west of Ryogaemachi-dori. 🕐 Noon–2:30pm (LO 2pm)/6pm–10:30 (LO 9:30pm). Closed Monday. 📞 075-221-5570. @ www. cornorosso.net. 🚇 中京区両替町通り御池下ル

DUE ドゥーエ

Italian   D17

The large, stone Taisho 9 building (established 1919) has housed several enterprises: first a bank, then the American Center in the 1970s, and now an Italian-style restaurant, a gallery, and several shops offering goods such as essential oils from Australia.

Immediately to the left of Taisho 9's entrance is Due (pronounced "doo-eh"). Although Due's entrance has been remodeled, the stairway and polished wooden-plank floors immediately evoke the age and sturdy construction techniques that mark Japan's 80-year-old financial institutions. The wide thick-beamed stairwell gleams with polish and is another prime example of early Western-style carpentry. Inside, a counter that seats 18 takes up half the shop, and table-and-chair seating holds another 10 or so. Large leaded windows let in plenty of light to the restaurant, and the high ceiling makes it a pleasant, casual space.

A choice of pasta and a salad is ¥980, and the ¥1,500 lunch includes an appetizer, salad, choice of pasta, dessert, and coffee/tea.

➡️ In Fumitsubaki Building at northeast corner of intersection of Sanjo-dori and Ryogaemachi-dori, just west of Karasuma-dori,. 🕐 11am–2pm/5pm–11pm. 📞 075-213-3922. @ www.ushinohone.com/due. 🚇 京区三条烏丸西入ル

EN 圓

The elegant façade of this very attractive reno-vated 120-year-old inn is a bit at odds with its south-side neighbor (a movie theater with lurid advertisements), but one step past the *noren* curtain is a step into a gracious bygone era.

A stone pathway leads past a beautiful miniature garden with a sasanqua camellia tree, a weeping maple, and bamboo to the entrance, where shoes must be removed.

Most rooms have comfortable sunken tatami seating; one has tables and chairs. Exposed beams, bamboo sliding doors, transoms with wicker weave patterns, and soft lighting maintain a comfortably traditional ambience.

(For history buffs, Suya, an old inn where the young samurai warrior Sakamoto Ryoma [1836–67] is rumored to have stayed, is two buildings east. The first floor has been converted into a souvenir shop, and admittance to the second floor requires an entrance fee of ¥500.)

En is a beef restaurant, and even the ¥1,000 beef curry is beauti-fully presented in attractive earthenware dishes. The lunchbox menu with slices of grilled beef over rice comes with a small salad and soup, dessert, and coffee or tea for ¥1,500. More expensive lunches range from ¥2,000–¥4,000. Dinner starts at ¥5,500.

➡️ 1 block south of Sanjo-dori, just east of Kawaramachi-dori. 🕐 11am–3pm (LO 2pm)/5pm–midnight (LO 11pm). 📞 075-708-2100. 🚗 中京区河原町通り三条下ル 大黒町45番地

ENYA 円屋

Japanese   D22

The first floor of this former commoner's house
has been remodeled with
the kitchen enclosed by
a counter that features
sunken seating for 8. A
table by the front win-
dow seats 4, and another
table in the back tatami
room accommodates 3.

Shoes should be removed for all seating except the very front room
table.

    The fare is simple Japanese home cooking with a main dish, soup,
rice, pickles, and a side dish for the ¥750 lunch. With only 15 seats, the
restaurant is often full by 2:00 pm, so arrive early.

➡ Down alley on east side of Takakura-dori, just north of Nishikikoji-dori. 🕐
11:30am–2pm/5pm–11pm. Closed Wednesday. 📞 075-213-3451. @ www.enya-
kyoto.com. 🚗 中京区高倉通り錦小路上ル

FLOWING フローイング

Italian   D15

This brick and stone building dating from 1918 has been renovated
into an attractive café and restaurant. Featuring a distinctive cooper-
covered turret, Flowing is one of the few buildings in Kyoto with
awnings. This site was formerly the old Dai-ichi Kangyo Bank, which
was renamed Mizuho and moved north.

    A large open kitchen area lies to the immediate left of the entry,
which is fronted with cases of sandwiches and a selection of sweets that

can be eaten in or taken
out. Deli-like items are
available from 10:00 am.

High ceilings with
suspended lighting and
bookshelf room divid-
ers give diners privacy
without sacrificing open-
ness. The bank's original
inlaid tile remains near
the front door where the teller counters are now fitted with tall stools.
Otherwise, the floor is made of wooden planks. Tall street-facing windows bring in more light, while newer west-facing windows look out
onto a small patio with tables and chairs for summer months.

One remarkable feature is the bank's old steel-door vault, now
utilized for wine storage. Upstairs, a spa and "body studio" company
offers aromatherapy treatments.

Four selections are offered for lunch: pasta, a hamburger, a salad,
or a sandwich. Each comes with a small salad (the salad lunch just
comes with bread) and choice of beverage for about ¥1,000 total.
"Happy Hour" is from 3:00 pm to 6:00 pm, with draft beer for ¥300,
bottles ¥200.

➡️ Southwest corner of Karasuma-dori and Takoyakushi-dori. 🕐 10am–11pm. Lunch
begins at 11:30am. 📞 075-257-1451. @ www.flowing.co.jp. 🚗 中京区烏丸通り蛸
薬師下ル手洗水町645

GOGYO 五行

Noodles   D25

This elegant 100-year-old house was the property of a famous *geiko*,
Oyuki Morgan (1881–1963). When she was 21, Oyuki met the fabu-
lously rich banker J. P. Morgan, who was smitten and wanted to marry

her. But Oyuki, in love with a Kyoto University student, refused. After Morgan persisted for two years, Oyuki jokingly said she would marry him if he gave her ¥400,000 (about $1 million today). The banker sent her the money, which Oyuki

gave to her beloved, and she left Japan to marry Morgan.

Initially, the new couple lived in New York, but discrimination against interracial couples forced them to resettle in Paris, where they were freer to enjoy life as an exotic twosome. Ten years later, when Morgan died, Oyuki went to live in Marseilles with another man, and after his death, returned to Kyoto to live out her years with her sister here in this house.

Gogyo means "the five elements," which in Asia are wood, fire, earth, air, and metal—all of which have been tastefully incorporated into the interior decoration of this machiya. The front house has a large grill and bar with counter seating near the entrance. Additional rooms in the back house have wooden flooring. A modern inner garden has a glass-enclosed passageway.

Gorgeous hewn beams are lit up on the second floor, where there is table-and-chair seating. Slippers are provided for the rear area of the second floor, and, in the front area, articles and photos of the famous couple are displayed. Another reminder of the couple's extravagant lifestyle is in the building farthest back. The thick-walled storehouse (*kura*) has been converted into a bar with counter seating. J. P. Morgan was one of the world's richest men, and perhaps that is why Oyuki kept her wealth in a steel vault, which is now set into the floor of the *kura* and covered with thick glass.

You can get *ramen* dishes here, served with side dishes of pickles, for ¥1,500.

→ West side of Yanaginobanba-dori, just north of Nishikikoji-dori. ⏱ 11:30am–3pm/5pm–1am (LO midnight). Bar: 7am–3pm (LO 2:30pm). 📞 075-254-5567. @ www.ramendining-gogyo.com. 🚗 中京区柳馬場蛸薬師下ル西側

ICHI NO DEN 一の傳

Japanese

D32

A beige sake-dyed cotton curtain imprinted with a large *ichi* (the Chinese character for "one") hangs in front of this very large and distinctive black-walled building. Ichi no Den is a shop as well as a restaurant

that specializes in miso-flavored fish. Sales counters are just inside the entrance. In the restaurant upstairs, one can enjoy seasonal culinary treats in a gorgeous traditional setting.

The 100-year-old shop originally dealt in rice cakes but was totally renovated, leaving only the gleaming, massive beams on the second floor.

Immediately to the left of the sales counters is a waiting area facing the original inner garden—a beautiful bit of landscaping indicating the shop's prosperity. Individual rooms separated with half-papered lattice doors all have sunken seating. Lunch is ¥3,300 and beautifully presented on all manner of ceramic ware, the first course a selection of tidbits served on a long ceramic dish shaped as the Chinese character for "one."

→ East side of Yanaginobanba-dori, just north of Nishikikoji-dori. ⏱ 11am–2:30pm. Closed Wednesday. 📞 075-254-4070. @ www.ichinoden.jp. 🚗 中京区柳馬場通り錦上ル十文字町435

IL POZZO トラットリア イルポッツォ

Italian D5

This 100-year-old dyeing and weaving workshop has been renovated with an emphasis on allowing lots of light from the back garden to fill the downstairs. The exterior wall is a soft shade of red, an indication of the restaurant's Mediterranean-

style dishes. Shoes must be removed to sit on a raised tatami flooring with sunken seating, which can accommodate about 10 people. Shoes may be worn in the interior at table-and-chair seating for 3, and at the counter, which seats 7.

The suspended ceiling has been removed, exposing the older crossbeams, stained in a rich, dark color.

The ¥1,500 lunch is a bargain, with a generous serving of appetizers, homemade bread, a choice of two pasta dishes, an array of desserts, and coffee.

➡ East side of Nishinotoin-dori, just south of Sanjo-dori. 🕐 11:30am–2:30pm/5:30pm–10pm. Closed Monday. 📞 075-257-8282. @ www.ilpozzo.jp. 🚗
中京区西洞院通り三条下ル柳水町７７－２

ITADORI いたどり

Japanese D33

Featuring Japanese cuisine, Itadori is named after sorrel, an edible plant that is also the theme of a well-known Japanese children's song. Access to the restaurant is down a long, narrow, wooden walkway. An orange *noren* curtain hangs over the passageway, and a menu is displayed at the entrance to this 120-year-old home.

Set behind other houses, a house like this was rarely a commercial establishment, as can be seen in the lack of a *mise-no-ma* (room for a shop). Indeed, Itadori was the former residence of a dance teacher. One large room is downstairs, with counter seating for 7 by the kitchen and another smaller counter seating 3 facing the small back garden. A scroll with a single stroke of calligraphy hangs on the earthen wall. The two upstairs tatami rooms are attractively decorated with standing screens of calligraphy. Low lantern lighting gives the small space warmth and charm.

Itadori's specialties are free-range chicken and eggs. Their most popular lunch is *oyako-donburi* chicken and egg on rice for ¥1,000. The ¥1,500 *itadori ohiru-gohan* lunch is many small dishes, as shown on the menu, and the ¥1,800 *kisetsu hiru-gohan* is a very large egg roll as a main course with a few seasonal dishes and soup, rice, and pickles.

➡️ West side of Fuyacho-dori, just north of Nishikikoji-dori. 🕐 11:30am–2pm (LO 1:30pm)/5pm–11pm (LO 10:30pm). 📞 075-221-3976. @ www.itadori.co.jp. 🚪 中
中京区麩屋町錦小路上ル

KATSUKURA かつくら

Japanese   D41

The main store of a well-known pork cutlet chain, this structure was originally a large townhouse behind a store that fronted Sanjo-dori. Redone in the mid-1990s, it is now accessible through a lighted walkway with several large steppingstones marking the approach to the main entrance. A short *noren* curtain hangs in front of the shop on Sanjo-dori, along with a colored poster displaying the cuisine. Shoes may be worn inside.

Large beams traverse the ceiling, and the main room has a large circular counter with table-and-chair seating. A smaller room with four tables and a low window overlooks the Tensho-ji temple parking lot. The management has retained the soft clay walls and *shoji* windows, but most of the building was gutted to allow room for about 50 diners.

While waiting for their order, customers receive a small ceramic mortar and bowl to grind sesame seeds. Tables are set with two sauces for the deep-fried pork cutlet and citrus-flavored dressing for a shredded cabbage salad. A container with extra rice comes with the food, and you can request additional shredded cabbage. An English menu is available.

The warm and casual atmosphere and lunch starting at ¥1,200 make this one of Kyoto's more popular eateries.

➡ Down passageway on north side of covered part of Sanjo-dori, just west of Kawaramachi-dori. 🕐 11:30am–10pm (LO 9:30pm). 📞 075-212-3581. @ www. fukunaga-tf.com/katsukura. 🏠 三条本店 中京区三条通寺町東入ル石橋町16番地

KICHIJOJO 吉上上

The dark lattice front-
age and red *noren* curtain
present an attractive face
on this 100-year-old *chu-
nikai* (one-and-a-half-
story house). A white
lantern hangs to the left
of the entrance, and a
menu of the Japanese
dishes offered within is
mounted on a stand outside.

   Kichijojo (roughly translated as "the best fortune") was recently
established by a former chef of a major Kyoto hotel. His dream was to
offer *kaiseki*, classic Japanese cuisine, in a traditional setting. Smooth,
dark beams and wooden flooring buffed to a soft sheen, white plaster
walls, and a copse of delicate bamboo in the inner garden graciously
complement the atmosphere of this elegant old townhouse.

   The ¥1,200 mini-*kaiseki* lunch, beautifully presented on lacquered trays, is a delightful way to sample some of Kyoto's seasonal
best. Table-and-chair seating is available on both floors.

➡ West side of Yanaginobanba-dori, just south of Rokkaku-dori. ⏱ 11:30am–
2pm/5:30pm–10pm. Closed Monday (Tuesday if Monday is a national holiday). 📞
075-241-7576. 🏠 中京区柳馬場通六角下ル

KILALA きらら

Kilala is a word that means "sparkling," perhaps in reference to Kirara-
zaka, a mica-embedded slope leading up Mt. Hiei to the temple

complex of Enryaku-ji. One thousand years ago, the monks from this temple stormed down the mountain path to make demands of the emperor and establish their position at court. Today the route is greatly eroded but still passable.

Separate smoking and non-smoking areas are provided with the counter and large table, which seats 8 in the non-smoking side. Attractive narrow cylindrical paper lanterns hang over the central wooden table. The interior is light and modern in a modern Japanese style within this 100-year-old renovated Nippon Telegraph and Telephone Company building.

There are a limited number of daily lunch specials that start at ¥1,000 and a large selection of dishes in that range as well. When I went, the daily special was a selection of seasonal vegetables with a tiny portion of beef, miso soup, rice, and a salad.

See also the entry for Shinpuhkan.

➡ 3rd floor of Shinpuhkan building, on southeast corner of Aneyakoji-dori and Karasuma-dori. 🕐 11am–11pm. 📞 075-256-8081. @ www.shinpuhkan.jp/category/restaurant/kilala. 🏠 中京区烏丸通り姉小路下ル場之町

KIN NO TSUBASA 金の翼

Korean   D23

This 80-year-old commoner's house is long and narrow with seating along the counter and a small raised tatami seating area upstairs. The interior is a blend of rustic Japanese and folksy Korean decor. The restaurant has a gas torch outside and plenty of signs with photos of dishes.

Bulgogi is the Korean name for Korean barbeque, and many hot rice dishes with pickled *kimchi* toppings are on the menu. There are some innovative dishes, like cheese *chige*, a kind of Korean pancake with cheese blended into the

mix. The food is reasonably priced and hearty. Lunch is from ¥780.

➡️ West side of Takakura-dori, north of Shijo-dori (east side of Daimaru Department Store). 🕐 11am–3:30pm/5pm–11:30pm (LO 11pm). 📞 075-703-3229. 🚗 中京区 四条通り高倉上ル錦市場入り口下ル

KOKOROYA こころ屋

Japanese	D38

Two of the most attractive features of this 120-year-old converted *chu-nikai* (one-and-a-half-story house) are its exterior and the alluring selection of vegetables that sits outside the railing fence. The dark exterior with lattice windows

and a sliding lattice door offer passersby an inviting mien. A clay figure of Shoki-san, the demon-queller deity, sits on the narrow tiled ledge, warding off misfortune.

Shoes must be removed, as seating is at low tables on tatami flooring. The second-floor ceiling of this one-and-a-half-story building slants down, making those near the windows bend low to reach their seats.

A rather glamorous chandelier hangs above oversized chairs in a north room that allows a party of 4 a bit of privacy. But Kokoraya ("the restaurant with a heart") is more about good value *obanzai* (country-style) food than privacy. The one-tray ¥980 lunch has either fish or meat, while the ¥1,280 lunch has both. Lunch also includes soup, a small salad, a boiled vegetable, and two vegetables tempura style, which is why Kokoraya is one of the city's great bargains and often noisy with appreciative eaters.

➡️ East side of Gokomachi-dori, just south of Sanjo-dori (there is another Kokoroya on Sanjo-dori). 🕐 6pm–midnight (opens 5pm on Saturday, Sunday, and holidays). 📞 075-211-3348. @ kokoraya.moss-co-ltd.com. 🚗 中京区御幸町通り三条下ルえびや町332

KOSENDO 光泉洞

Japanese   D24

This very popular restaurant is known for its homey atmosphere and the homemade quality of its dishes. A *noren* curtain hangs outside this ochre-colored *chu-nikai* (one-and-a-half-story house), a wooden fence encloses the front, and a

long *mushiko-mado* window spans the second floor.

Upstairs, the suspended ceiling has been removed to expose overhead beams that have been cleaned and restained a warm brown, accenting the soft-colored clay walls. The half-frosted windows (a feature seen in many homes in the closely packed neighborhoods of Kyoto) are an attractive means of letting in sunlight while maintaining privacy. In warmer months, the windows are opened to offer a view of the treetops in the inner garden.

The street side of the downstairs and upstairs areas has table-and-chair seating, but the rest of the house has tatami flooring that requires removing shoes. The downstairs also features a *tokonoma* alcove in the back room with a view of the garden.

A chalkboard outside lists the daily menu and prices. Dishes are served on traditional pottery. A main course including vegetables, rice, soup, and pickles is usually less than ¥1,000.

➡ South side of Aneyakoji-dori, just east of Sakaimachi-dori. 🕐 11:30am–2pm. Tea time: 2pm–4pm. Closed Sunday and holidays. 📞 075-241-7377. @ www.wao.or.jp/user/suwa9448/englishsite2/index. 🏠 中京区姉小路通り堺町東入ル南側

KUSABI くさび

Japanese   D16

Kusabi's façade has been renovated, but the lattice windows on the first and second floors and the narrow eave with roofing tiles are very typical of a traditional home. A *noren* curtain hangs outside the entrance, and a large slice of wood above the eave announces the restaurant's name in *hiragana* script.

The first floor is mainly counter seating, with one small back room featuring sunken seating. Upstairs are two rooms: a tatami one in back with seating for 8, and a front room with sunken seating for a small group. The extended *tokonoma* has a flower arrangement in one half and shelves with delicate sliding door shelves in the other. The walls are clay, and light comes from east- and west-facing windows.

The traditional fare is based on seasonal ingredients, but a simple lunch might be sushi and noodles, pork, or fish as a main dish, with sides of soup and rice, for under ¥1,000 total.

➡️ West side of Ryogaemachi-dori, just south of Oike-dori, 1 block west of Karasuma-dori. 🕐 11:30am–1:30pm/5:30pm–11pm (LO 10:30pm). 📞 075-222-7770. @ www.kusabi.info. 🏠 中京区両替町通姉小路上ル柿本町404-6

KYOTOMI-AN 京富庵

Japanese   D4

Behind the white *noren* curtain and menu stand at the entrance of Kyotomi-an is a long, narrow, neatly laid stone path leading to a house behind a house and garden. An unstained wooden door contrasts nicely with the dark-stained frontage of this 100-year-old two-story townhouse, and the  traditional front garden has been replaced with a modern, minimalistic stone and gravel area that allows light and fresh air to fill the interior.

The front room has table-and-chair seating for 6 to 8 as well as counter seating for 6, while the upstairs tatami room has two tradi-tional-style low tables seating 4 and 6. Both floors have an elaborate *tokonoma* with staggered shelves, the lavish use of space a sign of the restaurateur's wealth.

Kyotomi-an's specialty is chicken dishes, and the ¥1,000 lunch offers a choice of two rice dishes with chicken and egg toppings, chicken soup, red miso soup, pickles, and citrus sherbet for dessert. A full lunch course with separate chicken dishes (*Nishiki*)—raw, boiled, and grilled—is ¥2,000.

➡ Down passageway on west side of Aburanokoji-dori, just north of Shijo-dori. ⏱ 11:30am–2:30pm/5pm–10pm (LO 9:30pm). Closed Thursday. ☎ 075-211-1157. 🚕 中京区油小路通り四条上ル

MACHIYA YU 町家兪

Chinese   D29

The frontage of Machiya Yu has been freshly renovated with new tiles, a lattice window, and a sliding door entrance. Glass and wooden sliding doors are used throughout, and the white plastered walls and age-darkened exposed beams lend the space a

distinct townhouse feel. One of the only non-Japanese design features is a large wooden Chinese medallion hanging from the high ceiling.

A beautiful inner garden original to the house separates the front and back buildings. The restaurant seats about 50, with table-and-chair and counter seating on the first floor and sunken seating on borderless tatami mats on the second.

Tasty and reasonably priced Western-style one-platter lunches start at ¥850.

➡️ West side of Yanaginobanba-dori, just south of Oike-dori. 🕐 11:30am–2pm/5:30pm–10pm (LO 9pm). 📞 075-777-2525. @ www.ab.auone-net.jp/~machiya. 🚗 中京区柳馬場御池下ル

MAEDA COFFEE 前田珈琲明倫店

Café   D13

Established in 1869, the ochre-colored Meirin Elementary School was one of the first elementary schools in Kyoto. It closed in 1993 as many families moved away from the city center and newer, more compact compounds were built.

Maeda Coffee inhabits one of the old classrooms in the school.

Japanese have great nostalgia for their early school days, and several old schools in Kyoto have been preserved and funded by local citizens. The Meirin Elementary School compound has been converted into an exhibition space available to many of the students who attend art colleges in Kyoto.

Outside the main entrance to the old school stands a statue of Ninomiya Sontoku (1787–1856). He is depicted as a young boy reading a book while carrying a load of firewood, an indication of his childhood poverty. Having lost both his parents while young, he educated himself, eventually becoming a well-known and respected figure. Ninomiya is used as a symbol of diligence and perseverance, and his image is placed in schools around the nation to encourage children to study hard.

The creaky wooden-plank floors and lights with fluted glass

shades suspended from the high ceiling (similar to those popular when the school was built) give the coffee shop a quaint, turn-of-the-century feel. The building closest to Muromachi-dori to the left of the entrance was administrative. Its wide stairway and wooden banister were some of the first touches of Western architecture that Kyoto incorporated a century ago. The second-floor room, however, has tatami floors and is now used for exhibitions. There is a sports ground in the back of the structure, and several galleries, some featuring installation art, are open to the public.

Lunch and an assortment of beverages and desserts—some an interesting blend of Japanese and Western tastes—are available for around ¥500.

➡️ East side of Muromachi-dori, just north of Nishikikoji-dori (inside building, Maeda is down corridor on right). 🕐 10am–9:30pm. Closed Monday. 📞 075-221-2224. @ www.maedacoffee.com/tenpo/meirin. 🚗 中京区室町蛸薬師

MARUKYU KOYAMAEN 丸久小山園

Sweets   D1

A black, wooden façade distinguishes the first floor of this very attractively redone 130-year-old tea shop; the façade of the second floor is white plaster. The shop's rounded crest is etched on the upper part of the glass entrance door.

Immediately upon entering the shop, customers are aware of the fresh aroma of ground tea leaves. The tea bush is a type of camellia grown in China, India, and Japan, but the processes that render the

different beverages are unique to each country. Japanese prefer *matcha*, a slightly astringent powered green tea whisked into a frothy brew. On the 88th day of the new lunar year (May), the delicate top leaves of the tea bushes are picked by hand. The Koyama plantations are in Uji (a town southeast of Kyoto). Steamed, dried in a gentle blower drum, evenly cut, the leaves are then rendered into a fine powder with stone grinders. They are never fermented as are other teas, so the color remains a refreshingly bright green.

Koyama-en serves a variety of beverages, sweets, and *matcha*-flavored desserts in a café-like setting of light-colored wooden floors. The front of the tiny shop has a display case of sweets that customers select for the *matcha*-and-sweets set. The sweet is eaten first, then the tea, a delicate balancing of flavors that continues to please connoisseurs.

➡ West side of Nishinotoin-dori, just south of Oike-dori. 🕐 10:30am–6pm (LO 5pm). Closed Wednesday. 📞 075-223-0909. @ www.marukyu-koyamaen.co.jp. 🚗 中京区西洞院御池下ル西側

MIMADELI みまでり

Japanese   D21

This slim, dark wooden two-story restaurant illustrates how effectively space can be utilized in Japan.

A tantalizing array of fresh vegetables preens for passersby on an outside display, a hint of the simple yet delicious meals served within.

Inside, the bartender/chef prepares the dishes behind a counter backed by a selection of sake bottles. Two small tables for 2 are stationed beside the counter, and upstairs is a larger table-and-chair space that can easily seat 10. A smaller tatami room on the second floor seats another 8. According to the current owner, this room—which features a suspended wooden ceiling, rough plaster walls (painted black), and a picture of a dry garden landscape mounted on the west wall—was the living space of the previous owner.

Six choices are available for lunch, all just a little under ¥1,000. Diners pay ¥100 extra for coffee or tea, ¥200 for a beverage with dessert. (Pumpkin tiramisu was dessert the day I visited Mimadeli.)

→ Northeast corner of Aneyakoji-dori and Ainomachi-dori (1 block north of Sanjo-dori). ⏱ 11:45am–3pm/6pm–11pm. Closed Saturday and Sunday. ☎ 075-231-8902. @ www.the-la-mart.com/shop/mimaderi01.html. 🚗 中京区姉小路間之町木之下町

ODEKAKEBIYORI おでかけ日和

Japanese   D3

The name means "a fine day to be out." The first floor, now a car garage, was once a foundry serving this district of Kyoto where the city's iron tea kettles and cooking pots were made. At the stairway entrance to the café/restaurant on the second

floor stands a menu and photos of the dishes offered: simple Japanese home-cooked lunches and a wide variety of dishes from all over the world (the owner also manages a travel agency, which explains the international menu items and the pamphlets and travel books within). Farther east on the south side of Sanjo-dori is the Onishi Seiwemon Museum of iron kettles, and on the north side of the street is Kaman-zaya, a machiya restored in 2009 by the World Monument Fund and open to the public.

The front room has table-and-chair seating for 16, while the back room is tatami and can accommodate 18. This was once the family room with a large *tokonoma*, an elaborate *chigaidana* alcove with staggered shelves, and elaborate fretwork on *shoji* paper doors. The back south-facing room has been enclosed with glass doors through which the garden can be viewed. A framed picture on one wall depicts what the foundry/shop looked like 200 years ago. The present building is about 100 years old, and now that the suspended ceiling has been removed, the virtually nail-free joinery of the exposed beams is impressive.

One of the specialties here is a rice-ball (*onigiri*) lunch made with rice grown in the Tango district of northern Kyoto along the Japan Sea. Miso soup, a side dish, and pickles come with this ¥700 lunch. Other lunches are close to this in price with ¥150 extra for coffee and ¥200 extra for a dessert of mango pudding. The à la carte dishes are very reasonable; the daily lunch menu is in Japanese.

➡ Southeast corner of Sanjo-dori and Aburanokoji-dori. 🕐 Lunch: 11:30am–4pm. Café time: 2pm–5pm. Dinner: 5pm–10pm. Closed Friday. 📞 075-255-3399. 🚗 中京区三条油小路南東角

OKUDOHAN おくどはん

Japanese   D35

This 80-year-old home once belonged to people in the delivery trade and is now a popular restaurant serving home-style cooking. Outside the dark-stained lattice front is a display of vegetables, and immediately inside the entrance is a reconstructed *kama* (an old-fashioned hearth)

in dark brown tile. The *kama* was added to draw attention to the type of cuisine served—simple, old-fashioned home cooking—and it is still used for many of the dishes on the menu.

You must remove your shoes once inside, but there is sunken seating at the counter and table-and-chair seating in the back room facing a small inner garden. Upstairs is all tatami seating.

For ¥950 the Gokomachi menu, a sampling of eight tiny dishes of vegetables and fish served with miso soup and rice, was the dish most ordered the day I was there. For ¥1,280, the same meal came with coffee/tea and dessert, but most customers seemed to go elsewhere for dessert. As with most Japanese restaurants, customers leave the day's menu selection up to the chef.

The menu is in Japanese, but photos of all the dishes are available.

➡ West side of Gokomachi-dori, just south of Sanjo-dori. 🕐 11:30am–3pm/5pm–11:30pm. 📞 075-231-2219. @ www.the-la-mart.com/shop/okudohan01.html. 🚗
中京区御幸町通り三条下ル西側

OMO CAFÉ omoカフェ

Café   D34

Words carved into the old wooden sign in the entrance indicate that this 100-year-old shop (and a Tokyo branch) once sold flavored sea laver (*aji-tsuke nori*). The completely reworked interiors of both the back and front houses are innovative and charming.

Omo's exterior has a Meiji-era lantern hanging over the glass sliding doors. The black-walled *mushiko-mado* slit-clay windows above are a typical example of townhouse architecture and denote a centuries-old style of prosperous shops in this area of town.

A huge black money vault on the stone dais in the front room is more testimony to the shop's past business successes. The flooring at the entrance is thick glass over a piece of ceramic art; the rest is dark hardwood with table-and-chair seating.

What once was a stone-lined pathway to the back house is now the kitchen with counter seating for about 8 persons. More rooms are in the back, including one particularly interesting room for 8 within the old windowless storehouse. The inner garden is enclosed in glass, the huge root of a revered pine tree left to rest among moss and white gravel.

The upstairs rooms offer mostly floor but also some sunken seating, available to parties of over 4. The timber used in the storehouse is stained dark to match the overhead exposed beams. Hand-blown blue glass lampshades are placed low over the tables to highlight the beautifully presented dishes, all served on rough yet beautiful Shigaraki tableware, illustrating the aesthetic of *wabi,* or rustic simplicity.

The back storehouse has been divided into small rooms, and the private atmosphere is enhanced by low lighting, a pleasant departure from the fluorescent lighting found in many other restaurants.

Omo offers a daily one-plate lunch of Japanese food presented in French style for ¥1,500. Other dishes are usual café fare: pasta, risotto, and a curry dish, all around ¥1,000. There are also many kinds of Japanese-style sweets pictured on the menu.

➡ West side of Fuyacho-dori, just north of Nishikikoji-dori. 🕐 11am–10:30pm (LO 9:30pm). 📞 075-221-7500. @ www.secondhouse.co.jp/omoya2_cafe-top.html. 🚗 錦小路 中京区錦小路通り麩屋町上ル梅屋町499

O-MO-YA HIGASHINOTOIN o・mo・ya 東洞院

French · D19

O-mo-ya has been tastefully restored by the architect Ryoichi Kinoshita, who works to preserve Kyoto's beautiful old merchants' houses. *Omoya* refers to the house behind the building in which the business of the resident merchant, in this case, a clothier, was located. This business building facing Higashinotoin-dori has been restored by the owner of Second House eateries. Just to the south is the entryway to O-mo-ya. Follow the *ishi-tatami* stone path past the inner garden to the sliding-door entrance. Inside is the original well and pulley. Store your shoes in the old *mizuya* cupboards.

The room at the entry has been converted into a gallery; the tatami rooms beyond with their low wooden tables and floor seating form the original main family rooms. Three *tokonoma* alcoves with staggered shelves and cabinet are backed with the original clay walls. A strip of textured Japanese paper borders the walls to protect the lower delicate clay edges, a technique often employed in tearooms. Attractive old-fashioned glass lampshades bathe each table setting in an aura of light.

The two main rooms face a large back garden with two tall stone lanterns and some large trees that reveal the age of this mid-town dwelling. A newly redone room behind the kitchen has sunken seating; its wall papered with the pale blue and white check pattern (*ichimatsu*) favored in the Katsura Imperial Villa. (This room can be booked for parties of over four persons.)

Beyond the garden is a *kura* storehouse, again with sunken seating around a long, irregularly shaped wooden table. A modern raked gravel garden with a single slender tree brings in the southern light, warming the tatami flooring and imparting a soft glow to the clay-walled tearoom.

Above the storehouse's door is a shelf with small boxes bearing the Tachibana family crest. "Candles" is written on the far left box, candles and oil lamps being the only means of lighting in what were thick-walled windowless structures. The earthen oven, added recently and used only once, is an oddity in this otherwise authentic townhouse setting.

The second floor's massive overhead beams are spotlighted to reveal the fine joinery for which Japanese carpentry is known. Two long tables with sunken seating accommodate about 20 people for special occasions.

Even the restrooms, although equipped with modern facilities, retain the walls and vaulted ceiling of the original rooms. (The women's room originally housed the bathtub.) And as seen here, Japanese houses all had sliding doors and windows, with small metal or wooden rods inserted as keys or to close the door from within, a deceptively simple yet functional mechanism.

Kyoto vegetables (*kyo-yasai*) generously accompany the French food, which is served not with forks and knives but chopsticks. (Ask if you prefer Western cutlery.) The menu changes every two weeks. The presentation and culinary inventiveness are excellent. Lunch is ¥2,500 and dinner ¥4,200.

➡️ West side of Higashinotoin-dori, just north of Takoyakushi-dori (behind Second House). 🕐 Weekdays: 11:30am–2pm/6pm–10pm. Saturday, Sunday, holiday: 11:30am–2:30pm/5pm–10pm. 📞 075-241-7500. @ www.secondhouse.co.jp/omoya1iijima.html. 🏠 中京区東洞院蛸薬師上ル

ORTO オルト

Italian D9

Orto's one-and-a-half-story building is a typical *unagi-no-nedoko* dwelling, a reference to a home as long and narrow as an eel's nest. It features a modern version of a *mushiko-mado* clay-lattice window, a rounded opening with two horizontal bars. Incidentally, the name of its street, Koromonodana-dori, refers to a shelf holding priestly robes, an item of clothing formerly sold in this district.

Slim and trim, the downstairs rooms have been gutted so that the whole interior is visible upon entry, with a slice of back garden to provide natural light and greenery. Orto only seats 20, but its fine yet casual ambience and skilled chef have assured it of regular customers.

The ¥2,000 lunch has a luscious array of artfully arranged tidbits: seasonal fruit, vegetables, and delicate slices of raw fish, soup, a choice of pasta, and coffee and tea.

➡ West side of Koromonodana-dori, just south of Sanjo-dori. 🕐 Noon–2pm (LO)/6pm–9pm (LO). Closed Tuesday. 📞 075-212-1166. @ www.ristorante-orto.jp.
🚗 中京区衣棚通三条下ル

OTONARI おとなり

Japanese D44

This 140-year-old dark lattice-fronted two-story *chu-ni-kai* (commoner's home) has largely been left in its original state, except the walls, which have been redone with rustic straw-speckled clay, and the beams, which have been polished to a smooth, dark sheen. The space is tiny, seating only about 15 downstairs and the same upstairs. The raised tatami flooring has been

removed to allow table-and-chair seating on wooden-plank flooring on the ground level and upstairs. There is one tatami room with sunken seating on the second floor under a sloping roof. The *mushiko-mado* clay-lattice window has been left as is, but glass windows have been installed upstairs and down so that the restaurant can be heated and cooled without destroying its century-old charm.

The chef is from Wakuden, a well-known Japanese restaurant that specializes in *kaiseki,* and has recently redone the menu. The cuisine here too is *kaiseki*, served on a a small tray with delicacies in tiny dishes with a bowl of buckwheat and rice in a broth. The light and healthy lunch is ¥2,000, accompanied by salty soya ice cream for dessert. Reservations are advised.

➡ South side of street just east of Kawaramachi-dori, 2 blocks south of Oike-dori (south side of Catholic cathedral). 🕐 11:30am–3pm (LO 1:30pm)/6pm to 10:30pm (9:30pm on Tuesday). Closed Wednesday. 📞 075-231-9569. 🔲 Recommended. 🚗 京都市中京区河原町通三条上ル恵比須町534-39

PAPA JON'S NEW YORK EATERY

パパジョンズイータリー

Café D18

Shinpuhkan has two new additions to make everyone's mouth water—a luscious display of Papa Jon's own homemade cakes in the entrance and the aroma wafting from the classic copper and brass Gaggia espresso machine.

The restaurant can seat 40 with one large antique table that can seat 8 to 10. Other arrangements are for 2-seater and 4-seater tables in a casual relaxed atmosphere, or for 4 at the counter. The works of local artists adorn the walls to complement the comfortable interior.

The lunch menu includes homemade soups, salads, sandwich melts, quiche, pizza, and the New York owner's mother's meatball sandwich, all from ¥850 to ¥1,200. Dinner plates are from ¥1,400.

See also the entry for Shinpuhkan.

➡ 3rd floor of Shinpuhkan building, on southeast corner of Aneyakoji-dori and Karasuma-dori. 🕐 11am–11pm. 📞 075-211-1600. @ www.papajons.net. 🚗 中京区烏丸通り姉小路下ル場之町

QUARIRENGUÉ 火裏蓮花

Café D31

The *mushiko-mado* clay-lattice window of Quarirengué has been newly plastered, and large glass doors on the first floor brighten the interior with western light. The sign is written in Chinese characters that mean "the light behind a lotus," under which is the romanized name "Quarirengué."

Several residences share the alleyway of this *chu-nikai* (one-and-a-half-story house), which offers a glimpse of what the old neighborhoods looked like when they housed the city's artisans, workers, and their families. The aromas of home-roasted coffee, a variety of teas, and fresh muffins (¥100) waft through the tiny yet cozy downstairs. Remove shoes to go upstairs for tatami seating around a low table and two comfortable stuffed chairs. The high glass windows bring in eastern light while respecting the privacy of nearby residents.

➡️ Down narrow alley on east side of Yanaginobanba-dori, just south of Oike-dori.
🕐 12:30pm–6pm. Closed Sunday and on national holidays. 📞 075-213-4485. @
karirenge.exblog.jp. 🚗 中京区柳八幡町74-4

RANMAN らんまん

Italian   D43

Pontocho-dori is a narrow pedestrian alley east of the Kamo River, little more than an arm-span wide and one of Kyoto's most charming passageways. It is a *geiko* district, filled with former *okiya* in which *maiko* train in the performing arts to eventually entertain in the numerous *chaya* teahouses ranged along the alleyway. Pontocho really comes to life at night, so most restaurants are closed during the daytime; a few are open on Saturday and Sunday only.

Ranman, however, is open during the week and has been

skillfully renovated, offering reasonable fare in a comfortable setting. (The name Pontocho comes from the Portuguese word for "point" or "bridge," because there were so many bridges along this damp strip of property

centuries ago when the Kamo River frequently overflowed its banks.)

An Italian flag hangs out front with several blackboard menus whose dishes are written in Japanese; an English menu is available within. Attractive *inuyarai* bamboo fencing rests along the wooden front wall. Entrance is through the sliding lattice door.

Shoes have to be taken off, but there is table-and-chair seating on both floors and sunken seating in one of the smaller intimate rooms upstairs. The building used to be an *okiya* where *geiko* were trained; unlike long narrow townhouses, the *okiya* has many small rooms where the young women resided while studying the arts of dancing, singing, and playing the *shamisen*, a three-stringed instrument plucked with an ivory plectrum.

Lunch from ¥1,800 includes an appetizer, pasta, dessert, and beverage.

➡ West side of Pontocho-dori, just north of Shijo-dori. 🕐 Noon–2pm/5pm–10:30pm. 📞 075-211-8606. @ www.kyoto-Pontocho.jp/ranman. 🚕 中京区先斗町四条上ル西側

RATNA CAFÉ

Café   D2

A small, carved wooden
sign above the door and
another on the pavement
identify this café. The
exterior has wooden-
framed glass doors and a
mushiko-mado clay-lattice
window above the door.
Ratna means "jewel" in
Hindu and is taken from
the name of a shop in

India the owner used to frequent while traveling there.

Ratna's 90-year-old structure once served as an ordinary house,
not unlike the many existing homes in the area. The raised tatami has
been replaced by brick flooring. The ceilings and wooden beams have
been darkened and the middle room's suspended ceiling removed.
Two skylights bring in light to the kitchen area, and by exposing the
beams in the center of the house the interior is made pleasantly airy
and spacious. Plain dark wooden tables and benches and rich tan plaster walls with minimal decoration cast a soothing feel.

The back garden is inventive, with upright slabs of stones set in a
small mound of charcoal upon which greenery has been added.

Lunch is a choice of different curries, a small bowl of soup, homemade pickles, and *chai* for ¥900. Dinner costs a mere ¥200 more. The
menu includes some English.

Cooking lessons are held on Tuesday and Wednesday; information is on Ratna's homepage.

➡ East side of Iwagami-dori (1 block west of Horikawa-dori), 2 blocks north of
Shijo-dori. 🕐 11:30am–2:30pm/5pm–8:30pm. Closed Tuesday and Wednesday. 📞
075-812-5862. @ www.h3.dion.ne.jp/~ratna. 🏠 中京区岩上通り蛸薬師下ル宮本町
795-1

SAIKONTAN 菜根譚

A sturdy wooden sign-board bearing the name of the restaurant gives the building an almost solid, countrified feel. The 100-year-old shop used to sell sugar in all its forms from rock to powder and syrup, white as well as the indigenous black sugar favored by Japanese in traditional sweets.

Entry is through the hanging *noren* curtain on the left where the kitchen still operates, as can be seen from the large iron woks set on tiled hearths. A narrow stone-laid path leads back to interior rooms on the first and second floors. *Tokonoma* are in the rooms in the back-house (*omoya*), which has views of the inner garden. The original rooms remain tatami but use square, unbordered mats. Charcoal mixed in with earthen-colored clay blackens the walls, with bits of straw added, a technique evoking the rusticity of the countryside. Food, served on elevated trays, is an eclectic blend of Japanese, Korean, Chinese, and Okinawan dishes in a "*bento* lunch box." Dishes change according to the season and the chef's daily selections from the market. There is counter seating with chairs, but otherwise seating is on tatami. Lunch is from ¥1,500; *bento* are ¥1,800, and dinner is ¥4,000.

➡️ West side of Yanaginobanba-dori, just north of Takoyakushi-dori. 🕐 11:30am–3pm (LO 2pm)/5pm–11pm (LO 10pm). 📞 075-254-1472. 🚗 中京区柳馬場通り蛸薬師上ル井筒屋町417

SARASA KAYUKOJI さらさ花遊小路

Café D37

There are several Sarasa restaurants in Kyoto, all idiosyncratic in décor; casual and funky, they are perfect places to sit and relax over a cup of tea, trying one of the homemade desserts or the very filling daily lunch.

This Sarasa is a little hard to spot since it is down a narrow, poster-lined entrance behind the stores on the south side of Kayukoji, an alley. The building is about 100 years old and was formerly a noodle restaurant. The interior is dark wood with stool seating at the bar and a lounge area next to a small garden. Upstairs has exposed beams and plenty of light coming in the windows lining the lounge area. Bookshelves are filled with reading material, and Internet access is available. Despite the large interior, most of the small dark wooden tables only seat 2. The feeling is spacious and light and the menu hearty. While the English menu covers only the main items and lacks detailed descriptions, at these prices (¥800 for lunch), you can have a satisfying meal or snack and not be disappointed.

There are little "green" touches like reusable chopsticks on the tables and meals served on easy-to-wash trays. Hanging scrolls and old and new posters make up the interior decoration, and plain white globe lights keep it simple.

➡ Down passageway on south side of Kayukoji (an alley), 1 block north of Shijo-dori, just east of Shinkyogoku-dori. 🕐 Noon–11:30pm. Closed last Wednesday of month. 📞 075-212-2310. @ sarasak2.exblog.jp. 🏠 中京区新京極四条上ル中之町565-13

SECOND HOUSE HIGASHINOTOIN

セカンドハウス東洞院

Café D20

This eatery is one of the oldest renovated town-houses of its kind. Originally the shop belonged to a well-to-do *obi* dealer. The 100-year-old building was gutted and the flooring lowered to allow two wooden floors with seating for about 50

people. Huge beams have been lightened and windows added to give the interior a fresh and airy feeling. All tables and chairs are a light-colored wood to match. The first floor has a glass counter containing many of Second House's tempting selection of cakes. There is a café at the back of the entrance area, a popular place to spend a little time over a cup of coffee with a view of the rear garden.

Second House offers a very reasonable lunch set of soup or salad and a choice of pasta for ¥1,050. Coffee or tea is an extra ¥100.

➡ West side of Higashinotoin-dori, just north of Takoyakushi-dori, across from Wings. 🕐 10am–10pm. 📞 075-231-1717. @ www.secondhouse.co.jp. 🏠 中京区東洞院通蛸薬師上ル

SHINPUHKAN 新風館

Various Cuisines D18

Shinpuhkan was built in 1926, designed by the Ministry of Posts and Communications architect Yoshida Tetsuro (1894–1956) as the Den

Den Central Telephone Company (NTT) Building. The brick archways were considered innovative in a government building, and the site was registered as a Cultural Property in 1983.

The interior has been gutted and replaced with shops and restaurants and cafés along its walls. The structure's central area is now an open performance space; visitors may be surprised by the variety of groups and excellent talent invited to perform here. There are several restaurants on the third floor and a popular café on ground level. Those mentioned in this book are Ask a Giraffe, Kilala, Papa Jon's New York Eatery, and Tawawa.

➡️ Southeast corner of Aneyakoji-dori and Karasuma-dori. 🕐 Weekdays: 11am–8pm. Weekends: 11am–9pm. Restaurants: 11am–11pm. 📞 075-213-6688. @ www.shinpuhkan.jp. 🏠 中京区烏丸通り姉小路下ル場之町

SUGARI すがり

Japanese   D7

This unassuming old traditional house has backed its lattice frontage with glass windows. Reed screens (*sudare*), usually used during summer months to reduce the sun's rays and also for privacy, hang from the sec-

ond floor. The entrance, on the left, is a door within a door (*kuguri-do*) and leads back to a ticket-dispensing machine where customers select from the noodle menu, buy a ticket, and wait to be seated. Both times I went, there was a long line waiting for a seat at the 12-person counter. (Noodle eateries have a fast turnover and reservations are rarely necessary; customers simply wait 10 minutes or so to be seated.)

The house was built about 100 years ago with dark overhead exposed beams and a skylight, and where the old bath and toilet stood in back there is now a modern restroom. A small south-facing garden gives a bit of light to the interior, which has been completely renovated to include a clay wall with abstract design, attractive floor lighting, and a sleek one-plank wooden counter.

The main dish is *tsuke-men*, wheat noodles served in a pouring bowl and topped with a plump sweet leek and diced green onions. A bowl of chicken-based broth with pieces of fatty pork is served separately. Dip the noodles into this mixture. Although the wheat is imported from Canada, the noodles are made in Kyoto with no additives, and the broth is deliciously oil-free so the aftertaste is pleasantly light. When you finish the noodles, staff will ladle in some clear soup so you can drink the remaining broth. Powdered garlic, Japanese green pepper, and chili pepper are available on trays on the counter.

➡ South side of 1st alley north of Shijo-dori, just east of Shinmachi-dori (parking lot is on corner). 🕐 11:30am–3pm/6pm–9pm. 📞 075-205-1185. @ www.takakura-nijo.jp. 🏠 中京区新町四条上ル

TAWAWA タワワ

Japanese   D18

After Tawawa's customers are seated and select their main dish, they are given tableware and chopsticks and invited to help themselves to a selection of vegetables and dressings. All are identified in Japanese as locally produced. For example, the green creamy dressing was labeled as Kamigamo leek dressing, indicating that it is from the northern part of the city and in season.

The west-facing glass windows bring lots of light into the modern open interior. Seating for 60 is possible, and judging from the number of people waiting for a space, Tawawa is one of the more popular eateries in Shinpuhkan.

Kyo-yasai simply refers to Kyoto vegetables. There has been a bit of a craze over locally grown vegetables in the past decade, especially as Japanese have become aware of how much of their produce is imported. This is not to say that Japanese vegetables are the purest in the world, but the bar was raised after toxins were found in Chinese imports. That and pride in indigenous dishes spurred demand. Kyoto chefs then started to emphasize dishes that allow the diner to savor tastes that have existed for centuries. Typical Kyoto vegetables are *mizuna*, a dark green leafy vegetable; *shogoin kabura*, a turnip grown in the Shogoin district; *kintoki ninjin*, a deep red carrot; *ebi imo*, a kind of potato; and *kujo-negi*, leeks from the Kujo area. Radishes, Kikuna chrysanthemum greens, and tiny eggplants are others often found on the list. There are more, depending on the season, but these are some of the best-known ones. Restaurants claiming to serve *kyo-yasai* guarantee a more discerning clientele, not just vegetarians. The true taste of Kyoto is a seasonal one, despite all the hothouse coddling our gastronomic tastes have come to expect.

The ¥1,000 lunch from 11:00 am to 2:00 pm offers three main items: a salmon dish, pasta course, or curry. Freshly baked bread with bits of sweet potato and *kabocha* squash or rice accompanies the dishes. Dessert and coffee or tea are included.

See also the entry for Shinpuhkan.

➡️ 3rd floor of Shinpuhkan building, on southeast corner of Aneyakoji-dori and Karasuma-dori. 🕐 11am–11pm. 📞 075-257-8058. @ www.kyo-tawawa.co.jp. 🚗
中京区烏丸通り姉小路下ル場之町

USHI NO HONE うしのほね

Japanese   D36

This 100-year-old house has been renovated and given a homey, rustic feel. The dark interior has only one skylight on the northern wall; the five-table second-floor room is lit by south-facing windows. The rest of the suspended ceiling

has been removed so the main dining area reaches up to the underside of the roof, exposing the transverse beams. The effect is delightfully cavernous. Tatami flooring has been replaced with wooden flooring, but there is sunken seating at all tables and at the counter. Remove your shoes before you step up into the restaurant.

Rough clay plaster gives the interior walls a farmhouse feel. Bottles of the many brands of sake with their beautifully designed labels line the counter and indicate that Ushi no Hone has a following of well-imbibed customers.

Three choices were available for the ¥850 lunch: *omakase*, or whatever the house has prepared that day (the word means "leave it to us"); *oden* (different boiled vegetables in a hot pot); and a charcoal-grilled seasonal fish. All choices are hearty and delightfully varied.

Ushi no hone means "bones of a cow," a curious name for an eatery serving mostly fish and vegetables. The first owner who turned this house into a restaurant prepared French food by boiling the bones of cows to make soup and sauce stock. The present owners decided to keep the unique name.

➡️ North side of Sanjo-dori, just west of Tominokoji-dori. 🕐 11:30am–4pm/5pm–midnight (LO 11:30pm). 📞 075-213-2822. @ www.ushinohone.com. 🚗 中京区三条富小路西入

WHAT'S マツザカギュウワッツ

Japanese   D10

The black-tiled store-front features a menu on a stand and a large display window. The odd-enough name for a beef restaurant begs translation; nevertheless, this renovated town-house serves and sells the famous Matsuzaka beef, one of Japan's top brand name beer-fed cattle.

Enter the long, narrow, stone-laid path to the back entrance and you will be greeted and shown to a booth. Remove your shoes and put them in lockers inside the entrance. A sculpted wooden floor has replaced the tatami. Booths with sunken seating for 6 are on the first floor, and more booths are on the second. Each table has a grill in the center but most lunches are served on trays: a main dish, miso soup, and a salad. Serve yourself tea from the thermos on the table.

The interior walls are black, as are the curtains separating the booths and their cushions. Light comes from the inner garden, which includes a square pond with brightly colored koi.

Three choices of lunch are hamburger steak for ¥900; beef curry rice sprinkled with shredded cheese (a real cholesterol high) for ¥800;

and a pork course for ¥1,200. Two chicken dishes were also under ¥1,000 on the regular menu, but there are no choices for vegetarians (as is true in most Japanese restaurants).

With prices like these, What's is a popular lunch place for local merchants who need a real protein boost, so going after peak hours is advised. Smoking is allowed, but the separate booths help reduce exposure; however, after the businessmen in the next booth left, the air became noticeably clearer. Dinner is more expensive, around ¥4,500.

➡ West side of Muromachi-dori, just south of Sanjo-dori. 🕐 11:30am–2pm/5pm–10pm. Closed Tuesday. 📞 075-222-2989. @ www.k-whats.net. 🚖 中京区室町通三条下ル西側

YURURIYA　ゆるり屋

Japanese　　　　　　　　　　　　　　　　　　　D6

This former private residence, with its *mushiko-mado* clay-lattice upper windows and long wooden-lattice front-age below, appears much older than its 80 years. Old-fashioned wooden cookie-cutter door handles contribute to its

rustic and homey atmosphere. Beyond the white curtain is an inlaid stone path that leads to the restaurant, a large tatami room with seating for about 24. Another room, once a reception area, has two tables and chairs. The present kitchen has been replaced with a very modern one serving hotpot dishes.

Starting from ¥900, the lunch dishes are as tasty as they are generous and are served on large rustic earthenware dishes. The dishes are heated at your table; extra servings of thinly sliced green onions and a container of a rice and wheat mixture guarantee a very filling meal.

A low counter runs along the original east-facing garden. Upstairs the rooms have sunken seating except for one with a table and chairs.

➡ In nameless alley north of Shijo-dori, between Shinmachi-dori and Nishinotoin-dori. 🕐 11:30am–2:30pm (LO 2pm)/5pm–midnight (LO 11pm). 📞 075-231-4202.
🚗 下京区新町通り西洞院四条上ル

ZEZEKAN POCCHIRI 膳處漢 ぽっちり

Chinese/Japanese   D11

A handsome traditional lattice-and-stone exterior marks Zezekan Pocchiri as a once well-established kimono business in what is Kyoto's wholesale kimono district. The front room was for display and business transactions, and has a wooden

parquet floor and Chinese-style table-and-chair seating. Attractive sliding doors with oriental motifs impart an exotic atmosphere.

The rooms beyond this point were for family use; initially they were all tatami, but they have been converted into a sunken seating area, ideal for viewing the spacious inner garden with its large stone lantern. This elegant estate even has a two-story *hanare* or separate residence on its property.

All rooms bear the mark of a prosperous Kyoto merchant, with remnants of beautiful artwork in alcoves, wooden panels, and transoms.

The *kura* storehouse in the back has also been converted— into a bar named Pocchiri, after the clasp-like ornament worn by *maiko* on the front of the *obi*; a fine little selection of these are displayed in narrow glass-enclosed cases along the bar's south wall. The walls remain roughly plastered with massive exposed beams. Bold abstract paintings fill the tall walls on the side by the counter, leading the eye upward and giving the narrow area an expansive feel.

The cuisine is Chinese dishes served in the style of a Japanese box lunch. The daily *bento*, at ¥1,600, is one of the nicest meals in town. Dining at Zezekan will satisfy visitors on all accounts.

➡ North side of Nishikikoji-dori, just west of Muromachi-dori. 🕐 11am–3pm (LO 2pm)/5pm–11pm (LO 10pm). Pocchiri Bar: 5pm–11pm. 📞 075-257-5766. 🚗 中京区錦小路通り室町西入ル天神山町283-2

GIHAN EBISU-DO 魏飯夷堂

Chinese E4

This massive 140-year-old miso factory has been converted into a Chinese eatery. The hanging red lanterns outside and the stacks of round wooden steamers piled in the front window make it easy to spot.

The main structure of this venerable old workplace has been left intact, with huge dark-stained crossbeams featuring the kind of joinery usually seen in temple entrances. A collection of old plaster statues of the lucky god Hotei sits along the back wall, the lower half of which has been re-plastered a bright white to showcase the new scarlet ornaments.

Light flows through skylights in the three-story-high ceiling and from new sliding glass doors opening onto a humble garden area. This dwelling never had a proper garden, and today, a few potted plants replace a former storage area.

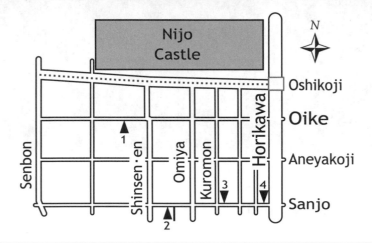

Nijo Castle

N

Oshikoji

Oike

Aneyakoji

Sanjo

Senbon
Shinsen·en
Omiya
Kuromon
Horikawa

1
2
3
4

E1 Omuraya
E2 Ran Hotei

E3 Sarasa 3
E4 Gihan Ebisu-do

Table–and–chair and counter seating for about 30 is broken into areas along the counter opposite the kitchen. The day I went, three lunch selections were available: tofu with ground meat, pork with vegetables, and shrimp with mushrooms. Each came with soup in a mug, pickles, rice, and two steamed ground-pork-filled buns for ¥800. Dessert, a bit of citrus sherbet, is ¥200 extra.

➡ North side of Sanjo-dori, just west of Horikawa-dori. ⏱ 11:30am–2am. Closed Tuesday. 📞 075-841-8071. 🚕 中京区三条通り堀川西入

OMURAYA　おむら家

Japanese　　　　　　　　　　　　　　　　　　　　　　　E1

A large, light blue, hand-painted wooden sign of a kimono-clad woman spans the front of this restaurant. Retro renovations are popular, retro in this case being the Taisho era (1912–26). The Roaring Twenties arrived and with them a newly

acquired taste for things Western. Rayon was introduced, and chemical dyes were used in interiors and clothing. A folk craft movement blossomed, affecting both household utensils and kimono design.

The interior of this 70-year-old building resembles nothing like modern Japanese minimalism. It's crowded, almost cluttered, albeit with a 1930s atmosphere. A beautifully restored garden with the original stone lantern and steppingstones leads back to an old *kura* storehouse that has been renovated to seat 6. About 20 persons can be seated downstairs with 5 at the counter; the second floor is tatami flooring for parties of 20.

The featured dish here is *omuraisu*: fried rice in a thin egg omelet wrap covered in sauce, usually ketchup but sometimes beef gravy. This specialty of the house is an apt reflection of East meeting West—a culinary example of Taisho innovation. Omuraya serves a variety of omelet-rice dishes as a main course with soup. Ask for the English menu. Lunch courses are about ¥1,000.

➡ South side of Oike-dori, just west of Omiya-dori traffic signal. 🕐 11am–3pm/ 5pm–midnight (LO 11pm). Closed Monday (or the day after if Monday is a national holiday). 📞 075-801-6950. @ www.omurahouse.com/omuraya. 🚗 中京区西ノ京池之内町１６－５

RAN HOTEI らん布袋

Café | E2

The stained glass door, and an etching of Hotei, one of the amply proportioned seven gods of good fortune, is a beautiful touch in this 100-year-old house. The traditional interior has thick darkened beams and is lustrous and handsome in the daylight that enters from the arcade side and back garden.

The solid wooden counter seats five, with a variety of old comfortable chairs arranged to give a homey atmosphere. A raised tatami area is for those who prefer to sit traditional style. The second floor is now used for tea ceremony lessons given by the owner, a Canadian who is a licensed tea teacher.

The façade has been changed to display the cakes available inside, a favorite indulgence of young women. There also is a good selection of tea (black and herbal) and coffee, regular as well as decaf, an unusual offering in this city. All cakes and sweets are made in-house. A beverage-and-sweets set is ¥800. Light meals are also available.

South side of Sanjo-dori covered arcade, 5 blocks west of Horikawa-dori, just past children's playground on same side. 11:30am–8pm. Friday: 11:30am–11pm. Saturday, Sunday: 11am–8pm. Closed Thursday. 075-801-0790. @ www. ranhotei.com. 京都市中京区上瓦町64, 三条大宮西入ル

SARASA 3　サラサ3

Café   E3

Sarasa 3 is named after its location on Sanjo-dori ("Third Street"). The 60-year-old tobacco store and residence was renovated and the tatami and suspended ceiling removed, giving the long and narrow café a spacious, open atmosphere.

Potted plants throughout the café and the back garden brighten up this otherwise dark covered arcade.

Beyond the back garden is a small house with tatami seating for 6 to 8 persons. The smell of freshly baked bread and cakes makes this a favorite place at tea time. A reasonable ¥1,200 buys a small salad with the simple rice or pasta dishes. (Newly opened and on the opposite side of the street is a Sarasa bakery shop with a large selection of take-out goods.)

➡ North side of Sanjo-dori, 3 blocks west of Horikawa-dori (along covered shopping street arcade). 🕐 11:30am–11pm (LO 10:30pm). Lunch: 11:30am–2pm. Closed Wednesday. 📞 075-811-0221. @ sarasa3.exblog.jp. 🏠 中京区三条黒門通り北東角

AJIZEN 味禪

Japanese   F3

Easy to spot with its unique stone arch "gate," this 70-year-old house was renovated in 2007. Immediately inside is a glass-enclosed room where buckwheat for the restaurant's famous hand-made *soba* noodles is ground in a giant stone

basin. White-clad chefs knead the dough into large balls, roll them out with a cylindrical wooden stick, fold the thin sheets over and over, and then wield a wide blade to cut them into fine noodles. Lessons in making healthful *soba*, Japan's favorite noodle, are also offered.

Exposed beams traverse the ceiling over the table-and-chair seating. A large *Nihonga* (Japanese-style painting) graces one wall. Chefs deftly assemble *soba* into hot and cold soups and other dishes at a counter in front of an open kitchen. In a back room, customers sit Japanese-style facing a garden with a large stone lantern and water basin.

The specialty is a ginger-spiced buckwheat soup, to which onions and pickles can be added. This lunch course also comes with a tray of delicious just-made noodles. Also recommended are the *umeboshi* (pickled plum) and the freshly grated *daikon* (radish) courses. Most dishes are between ¥1,000 and ¥1,500.

➡️ East side of Shinmachi-dori, just south of Bukkoji-dori. 🕐 11:30am–2:30pm/5:30pm–9pm. Closed Sunday and 3rd Monday of month. 📞 075-352-1051. @ www.ajizen.com. 🚗 下京区新町道仏光寺下ル

AMORE アモーレ

Italian F16

This *trattoria* looks like a New York transplant with its trendy lettering and outside seating. During one reincarnation, this was actually a car garage, so the front room has a concrete floor and the interior walls and ceiling are steel gilders that have been painted white. A rather elaborate chandelier hangs from the sturdy ceiling, giving the room a touch of glitter.

The back room has a painted white wooden interior with large plate-glass windows providing customers a luxurious view of the gulls and pigeons swooping over the Kamo River. An outside platform with table-and-chair seating is open in the summer months. On the second floor is the former residence, with earthen walls and a *tokonoma*, but the tatami has been replaced with wooden flooring and table-and-chair seating. Windows along the east walls overlook the river. Several decades ago, it was an inn, then a house with parking facilities, and

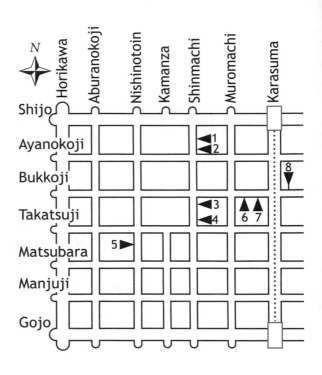

F1 Il Cortile
F2 Yaosada
F3 Ajizen
F4 Shunpuan
F5 Toute-epice
F6 Robinson

F7 Nagomi
F8 Sobadokoro Sasaya
F9 Uno
F10 Café Marble
F11 Misato
F12 La Table au Japon

F13 Cameron
F14 Baan Rim Naam
F15 Sumire
F16 Amore
F17 Bussarakan
F18 Shinkiro

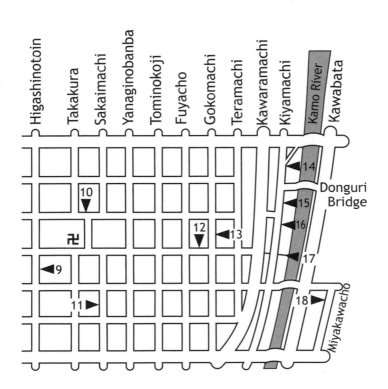

finally the café Amore. The renovated space has a fresh and open feeling, and the prices are reasonable. Lunch starts at ¥1,280, dinner ¥1,500.

➜ East side (river side) of Kiyamachi-dori, just south of Bukkoji-dori. 🕐 11:30am–2:30pm/5pm–11pm. 📞 075-708-7791. 🚗 下京区木屋町通り仏光寺下ル

BAAN RIM NAAM バーン・リムナーム

Thai   F14

The willow- and cherry-lined Takase River runs south along Kiyamachi-dori, a street whose name means "wood district," so named because from the 1600s dories carried loads of cut wood and charcoal to the kiln near Gojo and to the port of

Fushimi. For centuries it was a popular entertainment district with an easy command of supplies.

Baan Rim Naam ("house on the edge of the river") is easily identified by a standing Thai figure and many colorful posters outside the two-story building. The interior of this 80-year-old house has the long and narrow configuration of an ordinary house and a very fine view of the Kamo River. Exposed beams on the second floor and a warm, carved wooden railing give the restaurant a cozy traditional Japanese feel rather than a genuine Thai setting, but that is quibbling. The ¥1,000 lunches are tasty and filling, and the aromas quite authentic. Outside table-and-chair seating for an extra ¥300 is available on the riverside platform during the warmer months.

East side of Kiyamachi-dori, just south of Shijo-dori. 11:30am–3pm/5pm–10:30pm (LO 10pm). Closed Monday. 075-352-3823. www.rimnaam.com.

下京区四条木屋町下ル

BUSSARAKAN 佛沙羅館

Thai   F17

This riverside teahouse, or *chaya,* was previously owned by a tea-utensil dealer. *Chaya* are not long and narrow like the typical townhouse but were built with many small rooms used to entertain clients while they dined and were entertained by *maiko* and *geiko.*

With minimal changes, Bussarakan's Thai chef has converted the space into a comfortable restaurant with sunken seating in the tatami room and an extended platform (*yuka*) for outside seating from May through September. Low suspended ceilings, clay walls, and traditional paper sliding *shoji* and *fusuma* doors typical of Japanese houses make Bussarakan a casual and comfortable place to dine. After removing shoes at the entrance, customers are seated in the main room with its original *tokonoma* of exotic woods that shows the taste of the owner and builder.

The one-plate ¥1,300 lunch is a bargain of select Thai flavors, with ¥2,800 and ¥3,600 courses also available. Dinner courses range from ¥3,980 to ¥7,380, and there is an à la carte menu as well. There is a ¥400 per person charge to eat the one-plate lunch on the outside platform during the warm months.

East side of Kiyamachi-dori, between Takatsuji-dori and Matsubara-dori (from Kiyamachi-dori look for colorful signs with photos of featured dishes). ⏰ 11:30am–2pm/5pm–10pm. Closed Wednesday. 📞 075-361-4535. @ www.bussaracan.com. 🚗 中京区木屋町通り松原上ル

CAFÉ MARBLE カフェマーブル

Café   F10

This 90-year-old woodworkers' home has been converted into a first-floor café and a second-floor design studio. The kitchen can be seen through glass sliding windows behind the wooden-lattice front. After entering, customers can step onto a wooden-floor area with tables and chairs. On the immediate right is the former location of the old kitchen, with exposed beams and skylights three stories above. This well-lit area has table-and-chair seating. The two main rooms feature dark wood and face a back garden with an imposing stone lantern.

The back room, where the family originally entertained guests, has a *tokonoma*. Bookshelves along the wall offer all sorts of reading material (in Japanese) and a casual arrangement of old stuffed chairs.

The menu (in English on a chalkboard) features quiche, a variety of tarts, and sandwiches. The selection of four filling and tasty lunches includes a small cup of soup, a small slice of a tart, and coffee or tea for about ¥1,000.

The staff is young, as are most of the customers, who come to sit, chat, or browse the reading material.

North side of Bukkoji-dori, just east of Takakura-dori (across from police box and long white wall of Bukkoji temple complex). ⏰ 11:30am–10pm. Sunday: 11:30am–8pm. Closed Wednesday. 📞 075-634-6033. @ www.cafe-marble.com. 🏠 下京区仏光寺通り高倉東入ル西前町378

CAMERON 伽芽論

Japanese/Western   F13

This handsome building dating from 1880 was once a doctor's residence and practice. Extraordinarily large and substantial, it can accommodate big parties, making Cameron a popular place for weddings. Re-stained black *mushiko-mado*

clay-lattice windows span the front, and the third-floor addition adds an unusual architectural flourish. Long ago, third-floor rooms often served as fire-watch stations in Kyoto, especially in temples, which used their bells as fire alarms. Later, wealthy estate owners added a room or two onto their third floors to command a breezy view of the mountains and escape dreadfully hot summer nights. Elaborate tilework still adorns the roof.

The interior ceilings are high with black-stained exposed beams, and a back garden retains its original size and plantings. The *kura,* or storehouse, beyond the garden has been refurbished and re-plastered a resplendent white. It is now used for small parties, with table-and-chair seating. There are rooms on the second floor, but the middle second-floor rooms have been removed to create a more spacious atmosphere. Table-and-chair seating downstairs can accommodate 36 customers, and prices are reasonable. On a curious note, the owner named the place after the actress Cameron Diaz.

Lunch starts at ¥1,200 for a rice bowl course and ¥1,800 for the pasta course, and all meals are beautifully presented. (A popular place for wedding receptions, Cameron is usually closed to the public on weekends.)

➡ East side of Gokomachi-dori, just north of Takatsuji-dori (directly across from old elementary school converted into small museum). 🕐 11:30am–3pm/5:30pm–11pm (LO 10pm). Usually closed weekends for wedding receptions. 📞 075-351-2005. @ www.cameron-kyoto.com. 🚗 中京区柳八幡町74-4

IL CORTILE イルコルテイーレラ

Italian	F1

Long, narrow Kyoto homes are called eel's nests, and, as with this former clothier's home, often have one wide room with a passage-way leading from back to front. However, the present interior is very modern looking and doesn't immediately reveal the home's traditional roots.

The front sections of the first and second floors have table-and-chair seating, with a bar on the left behind the staircase. The inner garden is sunlit with potted olive trees. The back room on the first floor is tatami with a double *tokonoma* alcove and a traditional garden that can be seen through the *shoji*-paper doors. A large wood-inset Western-style table and six chairs make this a comfortably quiet room for a private dinner. The second-floor room has overstuffed

Naugehyde chairs, perhaps used for enjoying a drink rather than a meal.

The back room retains the flavor of a private home. The garden, with its stone lantern and natural light, reveals how families could retain their sense of privacy and lead quiet lives in the midst of a busy city. The long, narrow, eel's nest shape has been redesigned without sacrificing the intimacy of the original structure. The newly painted white interior brings a surprising freshness while eliminating the typical sunless rooms of the past.

The pasta lunch for ¥1,500 was inventive and tasty, with three choices offered: octopus with capers in tomato sauce; minced chicken and burdock root spaghetti; and scallops with rape blossoms and tomato sauce. Salad, a small dessert, and coffee are included in the price.

➡ East side of Shinmachi-dori, just south of Shijo-dori (almost next to Ikenobo Cultural Center; look for Italian flag hanging outside). 🕐 11:30am–2:30pm (LO 2pm)/5:30pm–11pm (LO 10pm). Closed Monday. 📞 075-344-0014. @ www.madoi-co.com. 🚃 下京区新町四条下ル四条町365-1

LA TABLE AU JAPON ラ・ターブル・オ・ジャポン

French　　　　　　　　　　　　　　　　　　　　　**F12**

Once used as a storage house for a nearby tea ceremony utensil wholesaler, this *chu-nikai* (one-and-a-half-story old house) turned its ground floor into parking for the utensil dealer and tastefully renovated its tiny second floor. The low

ceilings slant downward, so tall customers should mind the exposed beams. North and south windows and a skylight provide the interior with plenty of air and light.

The traditional white plaster walls, blue-painted beams, and parquet floor make for an attractive interior. A counter in front of the kitchen brings seating to a total of 14 customers.

The young chef, originally from Nagasaki, lived for years in the south of France, where he learned his cuisine of choice.

Lunch was an elegant repast comprising a choice of appetizers (I had salmon with wasabi dressing), a main course (scallops over a filet of white fish with charcoal-broiled vegetables in sauce), an innovative dessert (two scoops of homemade ice cream over a slice of plum and orange fruit cake), and coffee, espresso, or tea for ¥2,100.

➡️ North side of Takatsuji-dori, just west of Gokomachi-dori (look for blue and white exterior; paid parking across street). 🕐 11:45am–2pm (LO)/6pm–9:30pm (LO). Closed Tuesday and for lunch on Wednesday. 📞 075-361-6630. @ www.latable-jpn. com. 🚇 下京区高辻通り御幸町西入北側

MISATO リストランテ 美郷

Italian   F11

A white *noren* curtain and chalkboard menu at the entrance of this 90-year-old private house announces the restaurant's presence. The word *misato* means "beautiful old country," a popular sentiment for one's hometown.

The former residents were interested in the tea ceremony, and the street-facing room was originally a tearoom. A small sliding *nijiri-guchi*

door where guests entered for the ceremony is on the lower right wall of the front room. In traditional teahouses, guests had to bend low when entering the world of tea, a sign of humility. (The small entryway also forced samurai to disarm before entering.)

A stone path leads back to the main entrance of the restaurant, and a small covered bench where guests used to wait until the host was ready to receive them is on the left.

Shoes may be worn upstairs and down, as all tatami rooms have been replaced with wooden floors and tables and chairs. The sliding paper *fusuma* doors have been painted with a modern bamboo theme, but original glass windows remain in place.

A view of the spacious back garden with its original stone lantern and landscape design can be seen from both first and second floors. A small counter on the first floor can seat four and what was the *mizuya,* or preparation room for the tea ceremony, is now a large, glassed-in wine storage. The atmosphere is casual and provides a look into the former life of an elegant townhouse resident.

The ¥1,800 lunch comes with a beautifully arranged plate of appetizers, choice of pasta, coffee/tea, and dessert.

➡ West side of Sakaimachi-dori, just north of Manjuji-dori. 🕐 11:30am–2pm (LO)/5:30pm–10pm (LO). Closed Thursday. 📞 075-351-0098. @ www.mrmd.co.jp/misato. 🏠 下京区堺町通り松原下ル鍛冶屋町246-2

NAGOMI なごみ

Japanese/Western   F7

This renovated warehouse resembles a two-story home. The frontage features a handsome *mushiko-mado*—an attractive fan-shaped clay-lattice window. Inside, the long, narrow structure has sunken tatami seating to the right of the central passageway and a booth in a back room enclosed by *shoji* doors. Restrooms and the kitchen are to the left of the main walkway.

The menu is a mixture of Western and Japanese dishes, and the chef specializes in fusion dishes such as plum, beefsteak leaf, and clams on pasta on thin–crust pizza; mountain yam and salted fish roe; and Korean *kimchi* with bacon and cream sauce.

Ladies lunch was ¥1,600. Dinner prices range from ¥2,300 to ¥3,500.

➡ South side of Bukkoji-dori, just west of Karasuma-dori. 🕐 11:30am–2:30pm/5:30pm–11pm. 📞 075-353-5938. @ www.dining-nagomi.jp. 🚗 下京区仏光寺通り室町東入釘隠町242

ROBINSON ロビンソン

French/Italian   F6

This 120-year-old build–ing once belonged to an umbrella merchant. The interior is cavernous with a three-story-high ceiling of exposed beams where wet umbrellas were once hung to dry. The lattice front has been replaced by attractive

black-framed windows that are opened during months of moderate temperature to allow fresh breezes and natural light to fill the interior, a rare treat in midtown buildings. Robinson and another restaurant, Nagomi, are both just west of the house lived in by Buson (1716–83), a painter and renowned poet; a wooden sign stands in front of this notable building.

The window-enclosed kitchen lining the west wall is spotless, and a bakery on the premises supplies a steady serving of bread rolls. The stone step before thick vault-like doors opens to the windowless, lantern-lit *kura* storehouse. Table-and-chair seating doesn't require the removal of shoes, unlike the back storehouse room, which has sunken floor seating that can accommodate a party of 10 or 12. Comfortable wicker chairs are next to the rather large south-facing garden with its stone lantern, one sign of a prosperous merchant's house (*shoka*).

The restaurant's name comes from the story of Robinson Crusoe, a man who left behind his own familiar world to enter another. For today's Japanese, sitting in the luxuriously spacious room with such a high ceiling indeed may make them feel they have entered a different world, despite the very traditional architecture. Lunch is from ¥1,200 and dinner from ¥3,900.

→ South side of Bukkoji-dori, just west of Karasuma-dori. ⏱ Lunch: 11am–3pm. Café service: until 5pm. Dinner: 5pm–11pm. ☎ 075-353-9707. @ www.dreamwks.com/karasuma.html. 🚗 下京区仏光寺通り烏丸西入ル釘隠町238

SHINKIRO 蜃氣楼

Japanese   F18

Shinkiro means "mirage," and any of the young, graceful *maiko* who glide along the streets of this district present the spectator with a very dreamlike scene indeed.

The 85-year-old *chaya* teahouse has a black-walled façade with honey-colored wooden window frames and door, and a hanging *noren* curtain dyed with the name of the restaurant in stylized Chinese characters. The ceiling might be the most interesting feature: an undulating weave of thin strips of bamboo.

A menu on the wall next to the door lists a variety of ¥1,000 daily dishes. A more elaborate lunch costs ¥3,500 and requires a reservation, although most patrons in this old *geiko* district of Miyagawa-cho drop in for a quick bite.

Tables and chairs are in the back, and the counter seats about 6, bringing the total of seats to about 20 at most. Dishes are served on single platters that include the main course, a scoop of tofu, and salad, with soup and rice on the side.

The daily lunch was bits of different cuts of fried fish the day I was there, but most customers seemed to favor the single deep bowl of seafood on rice.

➡️ West side of narrow northbound street, just south of Matsubara-dori, 1 block east of Kawabata-dori. 🕐 11:30am–3pm (LO 2:30pm)/5:30pm–midnight (LO 11pm). Closed Thursday. 📞 075-541-0706. @ www.mrmd.co.jp/shinkiro. 🚗 東山区宮川筋 6丁目361

SHUNPUAN 旬風庵

French   F4

This traditional wooden-lattice-fronted two-story building has a *noren* hanging outside the entrance.

Although the flooring is of tatami mats, table-and-chair seating is available on both floors. The clay walls and alcove have been kept, as well as the small inner garden with its stone lantern. The atmosphere is restful and comfortable.

The menu, as in many of Japan's restaurants, changes twice monthly. The food is French, but with exquisite servings of seasonal delicacies served in courses just as classical Japanese food would be, delighting the eye and

palate. Rice and pickles are served last, as is again the case with traditional Japanese food. Lunch is ¥3,800.

➡ East side of Shinmachi-dori, just north of Takatsuji-dori. 🕐 11:30am–5pm (LO 2pm)/5:30pm–10pm (LO 9pm). Closed Wednesday. 📞 075-353-6008. rsvp Recommended. 🚗 下京区新町通り高辻上ル岩戸山町432

SOBADOKORO SASAYA 蕎麦処笹屋

Noodles   F8

This two-story traditional house is a little hard to find, but its very traditional appearance distinguishes it as one of the few remaining old houses in this district. A large side window on the east side is etched with the pattern of *sasa,* or

bamboo grass, a common groundcover in forests and gardens used as a remedial tea.

A white *noren* curtain hanging outside indicates that the shop is open. Upon entering, you can see the entire downstairs, with its gleaming dark wooden beams, counter, staircase chests, and spare back garden. You must remove your shoes to step up into the tatami room, but comfortable sunken seating allows you to understand how cumbersome Western-style furniture would have been in tiny Japanese homes.

Meals are served on crafted pieces of pottery set on red lacquered trays. Lunch starts at ¥1,000.

➡ 3 buildings east of Karasuma-dori on Bukkoji-dori, north on 1st alley on left, then left at parking area (restaurant is on left corner, northern entrance facing lot). 🕐 11:30am–4pm (LO)/5:30pm–midnight (LO). 📞 075-344-6708. 🚗 下京区烏丸通仏光寺東入ル上柳町３１

SUMIRE 菫

Chinese   F15

A long stone path leads to this elegantly restored inn. Its east-facing side is glass enclosed, allowing a full view of the Kamo River. Lighting is well designed, and touches of Chinese woodwork are used in the transoms and room dividers. The suspended ceiling consists of fine zelkova paneling, and zelkova tables and a fine wooden-plank floor enhance the soft natural setting. All dishes are served on solid white dishes and there are no round tables, a contemporary design.

The cuisine is Chinese, served in white dishes. Lunch is about ¥1,900, dinner about ¥6,000.

➡️ Down passageway on east side of Kiyamachi-dori, south of Donguri Bridge. 🕐
11:30am–2pm/5pm–9:30pm. Closed Monday and 2nd and 4th Tuesday of month. 📞
075-342-2208. 🆁🆂🆅🅿 Recommended. @ www.kyo-sumire.com. 🏠 下京区木屋町団栗
橋下ル

TOUTE-EPICE トゥーテ・エピス

Japanese/Western   F5

This two-story house has a distinctive face: menu items are written in roman letters across the glass window in front of the wooden-lattice window.

A solid wooden door has replaced the former sliding one on this 90-year-old building and opens to a ground-level entrance and a table seating 6. A slightly raised wooden floor has a counter with another 6 seats, behind which is the kitchen. Shoes may be worn inside. The second story's outside wall is plaster, as are the inside walls with wooden crossbeams, an architectural feature more often found in storehouses. The dark-stained beams imbue the interior with a soft, casual warmth.

The menu is inventive with many Japanese touches. The autumn menu included chestnut gnocchi and fig gelato.

➡️ West side of Nishinotoin-dori, just south of Takatsuji-dori. 🕐 11:30am–
2pm/5:30pm–9pm. Closed Monday. 📞 075-353-7778. 🏠 下京区西洞院通高辻下ル
高辻西洞院町801-5

UNO うの

Italian   F9

Instead of a *noren* hanging
outside, an Italian flag
marks this restaurant.
The old *kura* storehouse
was made into a gallery,
then re-renovated into an
Italian restaurant.

    Enter and climb the
stairs to the second floor,
where table-and-chair seating and a few seats along the small counter
can accommodate about 12 people. Windows have been cut into the
thick walls along the west and south sides, bringing in much light and
a refreshing cross breeze in warmer months. The menu features many
original dishes, especially some using vegetables and even a selection
of vegetable-based desserts. The daily lunch for ¥800 is a small salad,
pasta, coffee, and dessert.

➡ East side of Higashinotoin-dori, just south of Takatsuji-dori. 🕐 11:30am–11pm
(LO 10pm). Lunch: 11:30am–2pm. Closed Tuesday. 📞 075-756-4970. @ www.
kyoto-bar-uno.com. 🏠 下京区東洞院通り高辻下ル東側

YAOSADA 処矢尾

Japanese   F2

Yaosada's traditional lattice-fronted building has a low bench in front
with handbills of coming attractions and concerts, some of which take
place within.

    This area of Kyoto houses and maintains the large portable
floats used in the Gion Festival held every mid-July. The neighborhood is called Boko-cho or "ship district," since Fune-boko, the

Sailing-ship Float, is displayed here.

Inside the 100-year-old home, an inset stone floor has table-and-chair seating for 8. About 50 years ago, Kyoto's tram system was abandoned, and the gigantic flat stones from the roadbeds were given to citizens to use as they wished. Referred to as *ishi-tatami*, inset stone paths, they can now be seen in the fronts of houses and lining alleyways throughout the city, as well as in almost all the temples.

The tatami rooms upstairs are bordered with lovely thin-lattice paper sliding doors, and lots of *chimaki* hung on the walls. *Chimaki* are rice-straw charms thrown from festival floats. Originally they contained small sweets bound at one end, with the name of the maker written on a piece of paper attached to the outside. The ones thrown from the Kyoto floats, however, are now empty but are valued as charms against illness and hung in the entrances of homes to ward off disease and misfortune.

Yaosada serves a Japanese-style boxed lunch for ¥1,800 filled with seasonal produce.

➡ East side of Shinmachi-dori, just south of Shijo-dori. 🕐 11am–8pm. Closed Monday. 📞 075-351-3518. @ www.yaosada.com. 🚗 下京区新町通綾小路上ル四条町361

BAIWAN JUKUAIRO 白碗竹快樓

Chinese · G1

This restaurant's long name means "white dishes and bamboo chopsticks," and that is precisely what this Chinese restaurant serves up.

Located on the seductively exquisite stone-covered street of Shinbashi, in one of

Kyoto's *geiko* districts, the 100-year-old *chaya* (teahouse) was greatly renovated so that its elegant atmosphere could be retained. Shinbashi was one of the first downtown areas to be recognized as a historical zone, with some of the finest *chaya* architecture in the city.

A large white *noren* with the name of the restaurant in black is at the entrance. The exterior has a very unusual earthen-wall frontage with a lower wall of inset roof tiles featuring three wild boar. A large counter of thick smoothened grain sits 10 downstairs. Upstairs are several rooms, the back room with a *tokonoma* that seats 8 and the larger south-facing room overlooking the front garden, with table and chair seating for 12.

One of the specialties is shark-fin soup, served and priced by the gram. (A seven-year-old dried fin is mounted on a back wall, a decorative yet grim reminder of the way the sharks are discarded after the fin has been removed.) À la carte dishes of spicy *tantanmen* noodles start at ¥1,400, or vegetables and *ramen* noodles at ¥1,500 provide a filling and reasonable repast in an elegant setting.

➡ North side of Shinbashi-dori (4 blocks north of Shijo-dori) and 6th house east of Yamato-oji-dori. 🕐 11:30am–3pm (LO 2pm)/5pm–11pm (LO 9:30pm). 📞 075-525-0054. 🏠 東山区新橋通り大和路東入ル

CARA RAGAZZA

Italian   G4

Now an Italian restaurant, this impressive building began around 1920 as the Murai Bank and retains features of that incarnation, including a stone exterior and metal fretwork on the doors and windows. The building represented the wealth of the tobacco magnet Murai Kichibe (1864–1926), who popularized the modern cigarette by importing bulk tobacco (see also the entry for Chorakukan). Previously, Japanese had smoked small pipes packed with cut tobacco. William Merrell Vories (1880–64), an American architect, came to Japan as a medical missionary and designed a number of buildings, including a hospital for tubercular patients in Omihachiman (Shiga Prefecture) and Kwansei Gakuin University.

MAP G • Gion Area

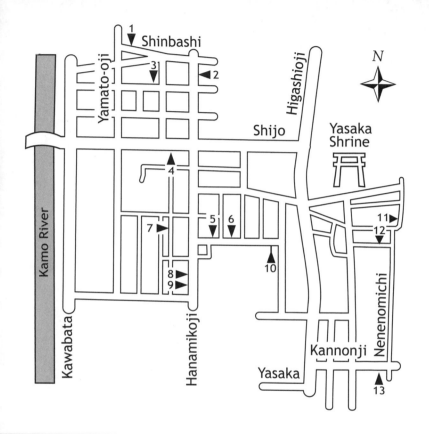

G1 Baiwan Jukuairo
G2 Scorpione
G3 Yagenbori
G4 Cara Ragazza
G5 Mametora

G6 Ristorante t.v.b
G7 Oku
G8 Taotei
G9 Karyo
G10 Hanasaki

G11 Chorakukan
G12 Minoura
G13 The Garden Oriental (Higashiyama Sodo)

Today, the marble floors and high ceiling remain on three floors with spacious rooms on the second and third floors for larger gatherings and weddings. On the first floor, a wall rack for wine sits behind the long counter where tellers used to work; the vault was removed and converted into part of the kitchen. The walls have been redone in elaborate plasterwork, framing two dyed works by the present owner.

Two waiters wear sommelier badges and can provide excellent information on wines to accompany a very reasonable and pleasant lunch, from ¥1,600.

➡ South side of Shijo-dori, just west of Hanamikoji-dori. 🕙 11:30am–3pm (LO 2pm)/5:30pm–10pm (LO 9pm). Closed Monday (Tuesday if Monday is a national holiday). 📞 075-532-5100. @ www.cara-ragazza.jp. 🚗 東山区祇園町南側 573-5

CHORAKUKAN 長楽館

French/Italian
G11

Filled with old-world charm—old Western-world charm, that is—Chorakukan, with over 100 years of history, is one of Kyoto's designated historical sites. Murai Kichibei, the tobacco magnate, introduced rolled cigarettes into

Japan in the 1880s (see also the entry for Cara Ragazza). Previously, tobacco was finely cut, tamped into the tiny bowl of a pipe, puffed two or three times, and set down. Cigarettes revolutionized tobacco smoking, and Murai became a millionaire. He started his own bank, and his prosperity allowed him to construct this art-nouveau-style estate to entertain guests. Many years later, it became a hotel for women. Even today the third floor serves as a hotel, and French and Italian restaurants and a café occupy the other floors. With its very romantic ambience, Chorakukan lives up to its name (meaning "the hall of long-lasting pleasure") and is a popular place for wedding receptions.

The stuccowork interior is elaborate and innovative for the time it was built in 1909. Crystal chandeliers and multiwood parquet floors accent the elegance of the rooms, and Japanese silk draperies and the plasterwork above the fireplace complement the floral motif of the family crest—curved branches of oak and olive—which is even depicted on the tableware.

The cuisine in Le Chene is French; lunch is from ¥4,000 and dinner from ¥12,000. In the newer Ristorante Coral the food is Italian, with lunch from ¥2,800 and dinner from ¥4,800. There is also a café open from 11:30 am to 8:30 pm.

➡ Southeast section of Maruyama Park (southwest of Yasaka Shrine). 🕐 11:30am–2pm/5:30pm–8pm. 📞 075-561-0001. @ www.chourakukan.co.jp. 🚗 丸山公園

HANASAKI 花咲

Japanese   G10

Hanasaki is a tiny *chaya* (former teahouse) where *geiko* entertained clients, located down a small alley. There is also an annex kitty-corner to the original building that offers more rooms, mostly tatami.

The softly lit rooms, low tables, and attractively papered sliding *fusuma* doors reflect an

atmosphere of age-old refinement. An elegant flower arrangement is in the entrance in front of a small glass-enclosed garden. The alley setting within the old theater district gives visitors a glimpse of a labyrinth that once harbored many a *chaya*. One can well imagine clients seeking out this kind of elegant, out-of-the-way place to relax and enjoy the kind of intimacy they sought during Gion's glory days.

The *bento* lunch is ¥1,800, and the cuisine is superb and authentically Kyoto. Dinner is around ¥3,675. Reservations are required, as is the case with all restaurants that serve *kaiseki*, or classic cuisine.

➡️ 3 blocks east of Hanamikoji-dori, then south on small street to just north of Gion Kaburenjo Theater. 🕐 Noon–2pm/5:30pm–9pm. 📞 075-533-3050. rsvp Required. @ www.gion-hanasaki.com. 🚗 東山区祇園町南側570-17番

KARYO 迦陵

Japanese   G9

This elegantly restored 100-year-old *chaya* (teahouse) sits in the heart of the most popular *geiko* district, Gion. The fine workmanship of the renovation features the smooth sheen of light-colored wood throughout the machiya. Sunken seating around  the first-floor counter can accommodate 14, with more sunken seating on the second floor. Radiating warm, natural light into the back rooms is a glass-enclosed inner garden with a spiral staircase leading upstairs.

The fine Japanese cuisine was rather exotic the day I went, when the first course was sea cucumber. But Western dishes can be arranged on request.

An eight-course lunch is ¥3,800.

➡ West side of Hanamikoji-dori, 3 blocks south of Shijo-dori (almost directly across from Gion Kaburenjo Theater). 🕐 11:30am–2pm/5:30pm–9pm. Closed Wednesday. 📞 075-532-0025. 🔖 Required. @ www.karyo-kyoto.jp/gion. 🚗 東山区祇園町南側

MAMETORA 祇園豆寅

Japanese   G5

In the heart of Gion is Mametora, a lovely 100-year-old traditional inn turned restaurant.

A simple white *noren* curtain hangs outside the lattice-window-fronted building. The entrance is also identified by a Japanese menu, a standing lantern set on the pavement next to the door, and rounded cones of salt on either side of the door—a ubiquitous Japanese custom that indicates purification and a repelling of misfortune.

Shoes must be removed in the entrance, but all downstairs seating is sunken, with 8 cushions along the counter facing the garden and 20 others at low tables. Old beams rescued from the renovation were innovatively installed as part of the counter. The inn's five upstairs rooms have been converted for dining use as well. The tatami is "bald," meaning without a woven fabric border, something seen occasionally in rustic teahouses.

The modern bathroom uses a large blue and white antique bowl as a sink against a black tile counter surface. Fresh flower arrangements in the entrance, main room, and even bathroom belie a spirit of Kyoto graciousness and old-fashioned attention to detail without being fussy.

Mame means "bean" and *tora*, "tiger," a humorous reference to the nine distinct, petite dishes of seasonal delicacies that are served with the ¥3,800 sushi lunch. Red miso soup and rice accompany this exquisitely prepared meal. Dinner starts at ¥8,000.

➡ North side of street just east of Hanamikoji-dori, 4 blocks south and east of Shijo-dori and Hanamikoji-dori intersection. 🕐 11am–2pm/5pm–11pm. 📞 075-532-3955. ᴿˢᵛᵖ Recommended. 🚗 東山区祇園町南側570-127

MINOURA みのうら

Italian   G12

Many inns and res-
taurants are scat-
tered throughout the
Maruyama Park district,
which abounds with
traditional architecture,
making distinguishing
a private home from a
restaurant confusing at
times. The appearance

of a *noren* curtain and a menu mounted on a stand outside (or both, as Minoura has) is the most reliable means of signifying a place as a restaurant.

The interior walls have been removed from this 100-year-old home, and on the second floor the huge overhead beams have been bleached and windows added, making the interior light and spacious on both floors. The first floor features views of north and south gardens. Tables and chairs on the first floor seat about 20.

The Italian cuisine is inventive and well presented. Lunch prices are in the range of ¥3,000.

→ North side of narrow street, south of Yasaka Shrine, 2 blocks east of Higashioji-dori, west from Waku-ten corner restaurant. ◷ 11:30am–2pm/5:30pm–9pm (LO). Closed Tuesday. ☎ 075-525-0909. @ www.yasaka-minoura.net. 🚗 東山区八坂鳥居下ル

OKU

Café   G7

Oku is located deep within the *geiko* district of Gion. A very attractive, dark wooden-lattice front has a standing menu outside.

A small pottery gallery can be seen through the lattice windows. To reach the dining area, enter and walk to the right behind the display. Solid white walls accented with magenta-colored seating sets off the beautifully arranged garden along the entire western side of the room. The minimalist design forms an exquisite background to the lush green of the garden filtered by natural light.

The café/restaurant is famous for its pudding, but you can just get coffee or tea if you like. The daily lunch is a very light serving of delicate seasonal vegetables for ¥2,300.

→ 1 block west of Hanamikoji-dori, 3 blocks south of Shijo-dori. ◷ 11am–7pm. Closed Tuesday. ☎ 075-531-4776. @ www.oku-style.com. 🚗 山区祇園町南側

RISTORANTE T.V.B リストランテ t.v.b

Italian   G6

This former *chaya* teahouse in the heart of the *geiko* district of Gion has retained its traditional frontage: a long span of attractive *inuyarai* curved fencing and dark lattice-covered windows. A menu is mounted on the stand outside the wooden-lattice sliding door and displays three different lunch selections, with all ingredients determined by the chef. There is no à la carte menu.

The cuisine is Italian yet presents customers with Kyoto's best seasonal ingredients artfully arranged and presented. The name stands for *ti voglio bene* ("I love you"). The tatami flooring has been removed to allow table-and-chair seating. White plaster walls interspersed with posts remain, and the added partition separating the two rooms on the first floor creates a bit of intimacy. Service is excellent. Including the second floor, t.v.b. can seat about 30 customers. Allow about two hours for attentive and gracious service for both lunch (¥3,500) and dinner (¥8,000) courses.

➡ North side of street 1 block east of Hanamikoji-dori, 4 blocks south of Shijo-dori, just north of Gion Kaburenjo Theater. 🕐 Noon–2pm (LO)/6pm–9:30pm (LO). Closed Sunday and 3rd and 4th Monday of month. 📞 075-525-7070. @ www.ristorante-tvb.com. 🚗 東山区祇園町南側570-155

SCORPIONE スコルピオーネ

Italian   G2

Located in the heart of
the *geiko* district of Gion,
this 140-year-old former
geiko house (*chaya*) is now
a fine Italian restaurant.

Scorpione's exterior
is fronted with a curved
bamboo fence (*inuya-
rai*) originally intended
to protect the outer
wall from passing dogs and carriage wheels. The *inuyarai* is a beautiful architectural feature that marks many of the traditional homes or
establishments in this district as fashionable and richly appointed.

A narrow path leads back to the entrance. The tatami flooring has
been converted to dark wooden planks, so you can wear shoes inside.
A waiting area with a beautifully painted wall of cranes and lotus serves
as a waiting room.

Straight-backed wooden chairs and tables are on the second floor.
Windows in the west-facing wall provide much of the light in the
otherwise dark interior. Removing the suspended ceiling has exposed
large curved beams, and a 19th-century chandelier adds a touch of
European glamour. A tatami room with full glass windows farther
back in the building provides a view of the interior garden with its tall
stone lantern. Beyond the garden, in the back of the house, are smaller
rooms where *geiko* might entertain their clients and are now available
for private parties.

The ¥3,000 lunch course is as ample as it is delicious. There are
choices of a main course and pasta. À la carte dishes are also available.

➡ East side of Hanamikoji-dori, 2 blocks north of Shijo-dori. 🕐 11:30am–
2pm/6pm–10pm. 📞 075-525-5054. 🏠 祇園東山区花見小路四条上ル東側

TAOTEI 桃庭

Chinese   G8

This two-story 100-year-old *chaya*, later a private home, is located in the heart of the *geiko* district and features attractive *inuyarai* curved fencing in front and a white *noren* curtain at the entrance. Most of the exterior architecture has been kept with little renovation. Table-and-chair seating is downstairs, and large tatami rooms are upstairs. The glassed–in garden has a stupendously large rock and water basin, a very modern touch to the otherwise traditional interior.

There are lots of noodle dishes to choose from the à la carte menu. The set lunch is ¥1,890. Dinner is a selection of non-noodle Chinese dishes, not family style, and runs about ¥6,300.

➡️ West side of Hanamikoji-dori, 3 blocks south of Shijo-dori (across from Gion Kaburenjo Theater). 🕐 11:30am–2:30pm/5pm–9:30pm. Closed Monday. 📞 075-531-2357. 🚗 東山区祇園町南側５７０－１２０

THE GARDEN ORIENTAL (HIGASHIYAMA SODO)

東山艸堂

Italian   G13

The former estate of the respected Japanese painter Takeuchi Seiho (1864–1942) is an extensive piece of property, with his old residence renovated into a restaurant and coffee shop. A wedding chapel has been constructed and provides young couples with a garden setting of native and Western plantings and a carp-stocked pond.

The thirty-six peaks along the Eastern Mountain range have long been a favorite setting for the villas and homes of many famous families, artists (like Takeuchi), and politicians. The eastern border of ancient Kyoto was the Kamo River, and the hills to the east were outside the original city grid; attracted by the scenic beauty, those who could afford it have often moved to these lush environs.

A dark rose-colored length of cloth outside the broad stone-covered driveway has the name "The Garden Oriental–Kyoto" printed on it; the path beyond leads up to the restaurant's entrance. The entire property has been redone, in places with distinctly Thai touches, but the outline of the original garden remains intact. Attentive staff wait at the restaurant entrance to greet guests.

A replica of the artist's famous painting of roosters decorates the wall in the waiting room. Table-and-chair seating is available throughout all rooms—and all have garden views. The Garden Oriental can seat 60 people, and rooms for larger gatherings are available. The room farthest back is a Western-style ballroom with molded plaster walls and leaded windows, but the rest of the building is distinctly Japanese with exposed beams in the central part of the dining room. A separate wing is used as a café/bar.

Lunch courses start from ¥2,600, and dinner ¥5,000. Reservations are advised.

➡ 3 blocks east of Higashioji-dori, at end of Nenenomichi. 🕐 11:30am–2:30pm/5:30pm–10:30pm. Weekends: 6:30pm–10:30pm. 📞 075-541-3331. 🔖rsvp Recommended. @ www.thegardenorientalkyoto.com. 🏠 京都市東山区八坂通下河原東入八坂上町366

YAGENBORI やげんぼり

This 120-year-old three-story *chaya* is located just south of Tatsumi Shrine and directly south of the narrow Shirakawa River, one of the most picturesque areas in Kyoto. Year round, egrets and resident mallards ply the shallow waters. In June,

locals gather to watch the delicate glow of fireflies, and lesson-bound *maiko* stop to make their wishes known to the gods at the shrine. The lane that runs north on the east side of the shop crosses a stone arched bridge leading to the shrine, the river, and the willow-lined Shinbashi-dori.

The black-stained lattice frontage has hanging reed screens along the second floor, a traditional way of providing shade for the sun-heated interiors and a bit of privacy. Shoes must be removed, but all seating is at the sunken counter or at the three tables separated by wall panels, allowing all patrons to catch the attention of the cook and watch his masterful preparation of each dish. The first floor can seat about 25, while larger private parties can go upstairs.

The restaurant's name comes from the *yagenbori,* a wooden grinding wheel set in a wooden mortar in which seeds and leaves used in Eastern medicine are crushed and ground. The implication is that all good ingredients, beneficial to health, will be used in the meal's preparation. An actual *yagenbori,* as old as the shop itself, is on the stairway shelf at the entrance, as is a woven bamboo screen with the red and white fans carried by apprentice *maiko*, indicating that they patronize this shop.

The huge old curving beam over the counter gleams with age

as does all the interior woodwork. Prints and brush paintings by the American artist Clifton Karhu (1927–2007) bring lush color with their convivial depictions of the Japanese epicure.

The Japanese-style mini-*kaiseki* lunch contains six small dishes with rice, pickles, and red miso and is ¥3,300. Dinner prices are triple. Eating in the Gion/Shinbashi and Pontocho areas confronts you with some of Kyoto's dearest prices, so inquiring about the cost of dinner before entering is highly advised.

➡ 2 blocks north of Shijo-dori,1 block west of Hanamikoji-dori. 🕒 11am–2pm/5pm–11pm. 📞 075-551-3331. rsvp Recommended. @ www.yagenbori.co.jp. 🚖 東山区祇園末吉町切通し角

AZEKURA 愛染倉

Italian   H1

There are very few farm-
houses in the city, but
the few that have been
moved to Kyoto feature
cavernous interiors held
by thick pillars and beams
that reflect the age and
girth of Japan's old forests
and the social standing of
the farmer. For centuries,
Japan divided its people

by job-defined groups, with farmers second only to warriors in pres-
tige, followed by craftsmen and lowly merchants.

Azekura was a *soba* noodle restaurant and kimono showroom
when its owner moved the 300-year-old Nara farmhouse to the northern end of Kyoto about 35 years ago. Now it is a fine Italian restaurant.
Large, colorful paintings warm the austere simplicity of traditional
Japanese design, while light from new front windows brightens the
mood and enhances the meal.

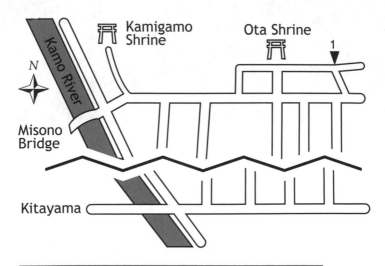

Kamigamo Area

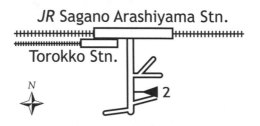

Arashiyama Area

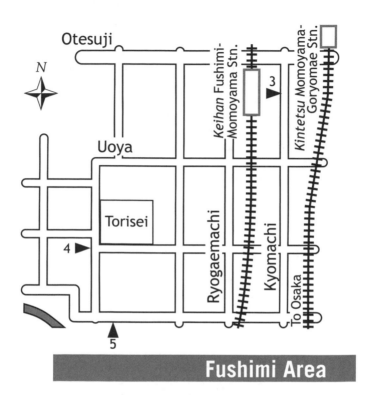

Fushimi Area

H1 Azekura
H2 Sagano-yu
H3 Juniya
H4 Tsuki no Kurabito
H5 Fushimi Yume Hyakushu

The surrounding grounds are scattered with stone images and rocks, collected by the owner and interspersed with moss, Kitayama cedars, and other seasonal plantings. Arrangements of cut flowers enliven the main gate and the entrance of the restaurant. On the upper level of the garden is another huge building, this one brought from the famed farmhouses of Takayama in Gifu Prefecture. Remove your shoes at the entrance to take a look inside this architectural treasure. Here, the walls are a stucco of clay and earth rather than the usual plaster. The sliding doors are solid, dark wood, and the entrance flooring is made of huge zelkova wooden planks. The upper rooms can be rented for weddings and large gatherings.

Inside the main restaurant is table-and-chair seating for about 30. The sheer spaciousness of the interior, interlaced with massive, dark-stained beams against the white plaster walls, has a distinct calming effect. Hard to find in any city, this quietly elegant atmosphere is perfect for a leisurely meal. Lunch is ¥1,500, ¥2,200, and ¥3,800.

→ Just east of Ota Shrine or 12-minute walk north of Kitayama subway station. ⏰ 11:30am–5pm (LO 2pm)/5:30pm–9:30pm (LO 8pm). Closed Monday. 📞 075-701-0162. @ www.azekurakankou.co.jp/ristorante. 🏠 北区上賀茂岡本町３０

FUSHIMI YUME HYAKUSHU 伏見夢百衆

Café   H5

Sake breweries abound in this area, with a number of sake-tasting establishments that allow everyone to savor the delicate nuances of local brews. The Fushimi Yume Hyakushu café provides the chance to sample sake-flavored cakes, buns, and ice cream.

The black-walled building was formerly the head office of the Gekkeikan Sake Company, one of Japan's largest sake breweries. Constructed in 1919, the office, with its high ceiling and open spaces, has been converted into a café with table-and-chair seating, retro lighting fixtures, and a creaky wooden floor (recently carpeted) that evokes decades of footfall by busy clerks. There are 17 brands of local brews available and sake-flavored sweets for sale. Cake and tea or coffee sets start from ¥600.

➡ Northwest of Gekkeikan Sake Museum, 2 blocks west of Ryogaemachi-dori. 🕐 10:30am–5pm. Closed Monday. 📞 075-623-1360. 🚗 伏見区南浜町247番地

JUNIYA 十二屋

Japanese   H3

Formerly a port, the Fushimi district with its pleasantly relandscaped riverside now boasts many fine restaurants, including Juniya. The area's springwater has made it a site for numerous sake breweries, whose warehouses add to the unique townscape.

Some of the breweries offer a wide selection of food to accompany the local spirits. Fushimi's history as a battleground in the 1868 clash between imperial and shogunal forces also makes it a popular tourist destination.

Juniya, roughly in the center of the Fushimi district, has a wide dark lattice frontage with a distinctive white plaster wall on its upper floor. The tatami has been removed and the floor lowered to accomodate table-and-chair seating for 30. Bringing in soft light and color, the north-facing garden just off the corridor has been preserved with a judas tree and azalea bushes.

The ¥2,100 lunch, an attractive array of bite-sized Japanese cuisine, is served on smooth lacquered tabletops and comes with dessert and coffee or tea. An à la carte menu is also available.

➡️ West side of Kyomachi-dori, just south of Otetsuji-dori. 🕐 11am–3pm (LO 2:30pm)/5pm–10pm (LO 9:30pm). 📞 075-612-7666. @ www.19an.com/jyuuniya. 🏠 伏見区京町３丁目１８２番地

SAGANO-YU 嵯峨野湯

Café   H2

Established in 1923, this former public bathhouse has been completely renovated while maintaining the original tilework and two narrow bathtubs, individual faucets, and mirrors. The central room has a vaulted, skylighted ceiling that provided light to the windowless interior and allowed the rising steam to condense and run down the sides of the slanting roof without dripping on bathers. The interior walls—even the massive beams in the upstairs gallery—have been painted white. Large potted plants add splashes of fresh greenery as does the maple tree growing outside near the covered seating area for smokers.

Old-fashioned elementary-school chairs with desk-like tables

can accommodate about 30 people. With its blond wooden furniture, dark-stained wooden floor, and white walls, the café feels
slightly Scandinavian, a bright and open place to sit for an hour or
two. Old shoe lockers hold a few *geta* clogs and other related nostalgic
knickknacks.

Lunch was curry rice for ¥1,000, or a vegetarian or chicken
sandwich in pita-style bread for ¥950. Coffee or tea was ¥300 extra
with any meal. Mouth-watering confections baked in-house are about
¥700–¥1,000. There is a Japanese tea menu featuring a beverage called
Gyokuro Saganoyu, an original blended tea for ¥950.

➡️ Directly south of JR Sagano-Arashiyama Station (on east side, set back from main
road). 🕐 11am–8pm. 📞 075-882-8985. @ www.sagano-yu.com. 🚗 右京区嵯峨天
竜寺今堀町4-3

TSUKI NO KURABITO 月の蔵人

Japanese   H4

The confluence of three
rivers, the Uji, Kamo and
Katsura, made Fushimi
a valuable port town
that connected Kyoto's
tradesmen to the city of
Osaka and launched ships
conveying the treasures
of the capital throughout
the country. Fushimi is
also the source of several
natural springs known for their use in the fermented rice drink sake.
After the warlord Toyotomi Hideyoshi built his castle here in 1594,
the population grew, giving rise to many breweries. Today, several of
these impressively large buildings have been converted into restaurants,

their thick walls, massive beams, and posts an indication of the prosperity and business acumen the brewers enjoyed.

Another product that requires absolutely pure water is tofu, and Fushimi has established its reputation with soybean curd products as well.

One place where visitors can enjoy tofu and sake is the converted brewery now renamed Tsuki no Kurabito. Cushions soften the sunken seating on wooden floors, and gentle indirect lighting creates an intimate atmosphere despite the size of the interior.

The cuisine specializes in dishes that include the local tofu and sake-flavored entrees. Lunch is ¥1,600 and ¥2,000.

➡ West of and between Fushimi-Momoyama and Chusho-jima stations on Keihan Line (opposite landmark eatery Torisei). 🕐 11am–11pm (LO 10:30pm). 📞 075-623-4630. ᴿˢᵛᴾ Recommended. @ www.19an.com/kurabito/index.html. 🚕 京都府京都市伏見区上油掛町185-1

Glossary

battari-shogi: fold-down bench attached to the front of the house used to display goods or accommodate visitors

bento: boxed lunch but, when served in a restaurant, an artfully arranged set course served on a tray and accompanied by rice and soup

buke-yashiki: warrior residence

cake set (pronounced: *kay key setto*): cake with a beverage

castella: type of sponge cake modeled on one introduced by the Portuguese

chaya: two-story building with many rooms where *maiko* and *geiko* entertain guests, literally, "teahouse"

cho: district within the city

choshoku: breakfast

chu-nikai: one-and-a-half-story house

donburi: bowl of rice topped with vegetables, egg, cutlets, fish, etc.

dori: suffix meaning "street," as in "Kawaramachi-dori"

fuchinashidatami: tatami mats without a woven border to evoke a rustic atmosphere, sometimes called *ryukyu-tatami*

fusuma: wooden-frame sliding doors, both sides of which are covered with a single sheet of thick paper; often opened to increase interior space

geiko: the preferred term for *geisha* in Kyoto, a woman skilled in the traditional performing arts

genkan: the entrance to the house where shoes are removed and guests received

giboshi-gata: onion-bulb shape

hanare: detached house on the compound of an estate

higawari: lunch of the day

hiru-gohan: lunch

hori-kotatsu: sunken seating at a counter or around a table that allows diners to rest their feet on a lower surface

ichimonji-kawara: wave-like edge of roof tiles

inuyarai: curved bamboo fencing in the front of a house. *Inu* means "dog," *ya* means "bow," and *rai* means "come." Originally meant to prevent damage to the earthen exterior of the house from dogs or carriage wheels, nowadays they are decorative.

ippin-ryori: single-item dishes or appetizers

ishi-tatami: rectangular slabs of stone often set at right angles to form a pathway

izakaya: Japanese pub specializing in small dishes, beer, and sake

kaidan-dansu: stairway chest

kaiseki: elegant traditional cuisine served in many courses

kama: earthen hearth

kami: spirit or god

kamidana: shelf in the kitchen where offerings to the household gods are set out

kawara: tile

kuguri-do: small door within a larger *o-do* door

kumo-gata: cloud shape

kura: thick clay- and plaster-walled storehouse

kyo-yasai: vegetables grown in the Kyoto district. Typical Kyoto vegetables are *mizuna*, a dark green leafy vegetable; *shogoin kabura*, a turnip grown in the Shogoin district; *kintoki ninjin*, a deep red carrot; *ebi imo*, a kind of potato; and *kujo-negi*, leeks from the Kujo area. Radishes, *kikuna* chrysanthemum greens, and tiny eggplants are others in this category.

LO: last order

machiya: townhouse or traditional Kyoto dwelling constructed of wood and clay with many evolved architectural elements and interior and back gardens; generally they are long and thin in shape and in the past serving a mixed use of business and residence. A *kyomachiya* is a Kyoto townhouse.

maiko: young woman studying the traditional performing arts in the *geiko* districts of Kyoto

matcha: powdered green tea

minka: farmhouse or commoner's house, with thatched roofs, mud walls, and large timbers for support

mise-no-ma: room in a house where business is conducted

moritsuke: attractive arrangement of food that contrasts color, texture, and shapes in one serving

mushiko-mado (literally, "insect cage window"): earthen or plaster window opening with widely spaced vertical columns—a decorative form of ventilation

naka-no-niwa: inner garden

Nishijin: weaving and dyeing district in west central Kyoto

niwa: garden

noren: curtain hung outside a shop to indicate it is open for business

obi: sash used to secure a kimono

o-do: main door

oden: winter dish of various vegetables steeped in broth

ohashi: chopsticks. A *hashioki* is a chopstick rest.

okiya: house in the pleasure quarters where *maiko* and *geiko* live and train

oku-no-niwa: back garden

okonomiyaki: grilled pancake-like concoction that includes vegetables and topped with bonito fish flakes and a sweet date-based sauce

omakase: Japanese expression meaning "leave it to me"

omoteya: front section of the house with access to the street and where business is conducted

omu-raisu: fried rice wrapped in an egg omlet

ramen: Chinese-style wheat noodles

ranma: decorative transom separating inner rooms

roji: alley or lane

sake: alcoholic beverage made from fermented rice

shinden: older estate style of building with low buildings connected by walkways and verandas with gardens and ponds

Shinto: indigenous Japanese religion

shoji: wooden lattice doors and windows covered on one side with a thin sheet of paper, some with a portion of inset glass

shojin-ryori: tofu-based cuisine

shoka: large inner-city merchant's house

Shoki-san: image made from roof-tile clay and placed above entrances to deflect misfortune from entering the house

soba: buckwheat noodles

sudare: reed blinds hung from eaves to deflect the summer sun

sukiya: "refined abode"; an earlier architectural style of less formal buildings with an emphasis on gardens and views

tatami: thick rectangular woven straw and rush mats used as flooring

teishoku: set meal of entrée, soup, rice, and pickles

teppan-yaki: grilled food

tofu: soybean curd

tokonoma: alcove, often with a decorative scroll or flower arrangement

torii: a "gate" or entrance to a Shinto shrine consisting of two vertical and horizontal beams made of wood or stone

tori-niwa: passageway through the kitchen from the front to the back of the house

tsubo-niwa: small compact garden usually in the front part of the house

tsukemono: pickles

udon: wheat noodles

unagi-no-nedoko: a long narrow Kyoto house (literally, "eel's sleeping place")

yashiki: estate

yuba: skimmed surface of boiled soy beans hung on sheets and sold fresh or in dried curls, a Kyoto specialty

yukimi-shoji: wooden lattice and shoji paper door with *shoji* panels that slide up to reveal the snow in the garden through a lower glass section

yushoku: dinner

yusuzumi: sitting outside in the summer evening to cool off

Bibliography

Coaldrake, William H. *The Way of the Carpenter: Tools and Japanese Architecture.* Tokyo and New York: Weatherhill, 1991.

Diamond, Jared. *Collapse: How Societies Choose to Fail or Succeed.* New York: Viking Penguin, 2005.

Fiévé, Nicolas, and Paul Waley, eds. *Japanese Capitals in Historical Perspective: Place, Power and Memory in Kyoto, Edo, and Tokyo.* London: Routledge, Curzon, 2003.

Kyoto Center for Community Collaboration, ed. "Machiya Revival in Kyoto" (in Japanese). Kyoto: Mitsumura Suiko Shoin, 2009.

Leaf, ed. *Kyoto Machiya de Gohan* (Meals in Kyoto Machiya; in Japanese). Leaf Mook (December 2010).

Mertz, Mechtild. *Wood and Traditional Woodworking in Japan.* Tokyo: Kaiseisha Press, 2011.

Moriya, Katsuhisa. *Kyoto no Ojikoji* (Kyoto Streets and Alleyways; in Japanese). Tokyo: Shogakukan, 2006.

Nishi, Kazuo, and Kazuo Hozumi. *What is Japanese Architecture?: A Survey of Traditional Japanese Architecture.* Tokyo and New York: Kodansha International, 1996.

Richie, Donald. *A Tractate on Japanese Aesthetics.* Berkeley: Stone Bridge Press, 2007.

Seike, Kiyosi. *The Art of Japanese Joinery.* Tokyo and New York: Weatherhill, 1977.

Shintani, Akio, and Jun'ichi Kanzaki. *Kyomachiya* (in Japanese). Kyoto: Suiko Books, 1998.

Totman, Conrad. *Green Archipelago: Forestry in Pre-Industrial Japan.* Berkeley: University of California Press, 1989.

Index by Cuisine

CAFÉ

Ask a Giraffe, 154 **D18**
Bon Bon Café, 107 **B4**
Café Bibliotic Hello!, 114 **C17**
Café Chobitto, 115 **C23**
Café Frosch, 85 **A8**
Café Hakuya, 85 **A5**
Café Marble, 212 **F10**
Cinq Ryokan and Café, 157 **D40**
Fushimi Yume Hyakushu, 244
    H5
Jujumaru, 109 **B1**
Maeda Coffee, 175 **D13**
Merry Island, 130 **C33**
Nunoya, 133 **C3**
Oku, 234 **G7**
Omo Café, 180 **D34**
Papa Jon's New York Eatery, 186
    D18
Prangipani, 95 **A6**
Quarirengué, 186 **D31**
Ran Hotei, 204 **E2**
Ratna Café, 189 **D2**
Ryokiden, 96 **A18**
Sagano-yu, 246 **H2**
Sarasa 3, 205 **E3**
Sarasa Kayukoji, 191 **D37**
Sarasa Nishijin, 97 **A7**
Sarasa Oshikoji, 138 **C19**
Second House Higashinotoin,
    192 **D20**
Very Berry Café, 145 **C35**

CANADIAN/JAPANESE

Le Pont, 127 **C28**

CHINESE

Baiwan Jukuairo, 226 **G1**
Gihan Ebisu-do, 201 **E4**
Ichi no Hunairi, 121 **C34**
Machiya Yu, 174 **D29**
Madam Koran, 128 **C24**
Meirin, 93 **A15**
Sumire, 222 **F15**
Taotei, 237 **G8**

CHINESE/JAPANESE

Saikontan, 190 **D26**
Zezekan Pocchiri, 199 **D11**

FRENCH

Ame du Garçon, 111 **C30**
Ao, 153 **D12**
Epice, 118 **C26**
La Table au Japon, 215 **F12**
Le Vieux Logis, 91 **A17**
Les Trois Maisons, 92 **A9**
O-mo-ya Higashinotoin, 182
    D19
Shibuya, 98 **A4**
Shunpuan, 220 **F4**
Tamaki, 141 **C9**

FRENCH/ITALIAN

ITALIAN

JAPANESE

Index by Name

Notes

Notes

Notes

Notes

Notes

_____

_____

_____

_____

_____

_____

_____

_____

_____

_____

_____

_____

_____

_____

_____

_____

_____

Notes

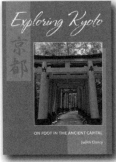

Exploring Kyoto
On Foot in the Ancient Capital
JUDITH CLANCY

Among the world's most cherished ancient cities, Kyoto, Japan, is perfect for exploring on foot. Richly detailed and small enough to fit in a jacket pocket, *Exploring Kyoto* is an essential guide to becoming an enlightened pedestrian in the area once known as Yamashiro ("the back of the mountains").

Exploring Kyoto offers 30 explorations, including the well-known—Mt. Hiei, Arashiyama, Heian Shrine, Ryoanji, Philosopher's Walk—and many hidden corners, spanning a spectrum of geographical and cultural topography, from bustling downtown quarters to remote mountaintops, from hip eateries to ancient shrines. Included are:

- Detailed maps tracing each route
- Over 30 descriptive photos
- Essential tips on etiquette and behavior
- Full index to all sites and attractions
- In-depth information on local history, arts, and festivals

5 x 7", paperback, 296 pp
PRINT ISBN 978-1-933330-64-8, E-BOOK ISBN 978-0-89346-991-7
In print and e-book formats at booksellers worldwide and online

www.stonebridge.com • sbp@stonebridge.com